HOME SCHOOLING

HOME
SCHOOLING

Other books in the At Issue series:

HOME SCHOOLING

Cindy Mur, *Book Editor*

Daniel Leone, *President*
Bonnie Szumski, *Publisher*
Scott Barbour, *Managing Editor*
Helen Cothran, *Series Editor*

San Diego • Detroit • New York • San Francisco • Cleveland
New Haven, Conn. • Waterville, Maine • London • Munich

© 2003 by Greenhaven Press. Greenhaven Press is an imprint of The Gale Group, Inc., a division of Thomson Learning, Inc.

Greenhaven® and Thomson Learning™ are trademarks used herein under license.

For more information, contact
Greenhaven Press
27500 Drake Rd.
Farmington Hills, MI 48331-3535
Or you can visit our Internet site at http://www.gale.com

LIBRARY OF CONGRESS CATALOGING-IN-PUBLICATION DATA

Home schooling / Cindy Mur, book editor.
    p. cm. — (At issue)
Includes bibliographical references and index.
ISBN 0-7377-1410-7 (lib. bdg. : alk. paper) —
ISBN 0-7377-1411-5 (pbk. : alk. paper)
    1. Home schooling. I. Title: Homeschooling. II. Mur, Cindy. III. At issue (San Diego, Calif.)
LC40 .H443 2003
371.04'2—dc21   2002070614

Printed in the United States of America

Contents

Introduction

Educational success is generally measured in terms of academic achievement. If this standard alone were applied to home schooling, most people would agree that home schooling can be a successful alternative to public school.

Testing evidence indicates that home schooling is highly effective in terms of academics. The average home-schooled student scored 81 points higher on the Scholastic Aptitude Test (SAT) than did the general population in 2000. At the National Spelling Bee in 2000, the top three winners were home-schooled. Studies show that home-schooled children also tend to score higher on basic skills testing than do public school children. According to the *Wall Street Journal*, "Evidence is mounting that home-schooling, once confined to the political and religious fringe, has achieved results not only on par with public education, but in some ways surpassing it."

However, one subject continues to surface whenever the issue of home schooling arises. Public school administrators, teachers, and parents are all concerned about whether home-schooled children are properly socialized.

Some of those concerned about the socialization of home-schooled children include those who had been educated at home but who later chose to attend public school. One such student, Trent Gist, was home-schooled until ninth grade and then attended a public high school. Gist believes that while "home schooling was great . . . it just wasn't for me . . . I know a lot of home schoolers who are very unsociable."

Gist's comments supply ammunition to other detractors of home schooling, like the National Education Association (NEA), who believe that public schools offer experiences and opportunities not available at home. They point out that home-schooled students miss out on the use of resources that encourage cooperation, such as laboratories, and activities that help develop teamwork and friendships, such as athletic programs and school dances.

Supporters of public schools maintain that public school students learn to work well with others, including those of differing backgrounds, and that they can achieve greater independence by attending public school. Negotiating the communal spaces of schoolyard, classroom, athletic field, and laboratory prepares them for "real world" experiences, they contend. Critics of home schooling believe that home-schooled children miss out on these important opportunities.

Without the chance to interact with those of diverse backgrounds, critics are concerned that home-schooled students will fail to appreciate and understand one of the core values of American life: to tolerate and appreciate the differences between cultures or groups and among individuals. They fear that isolation breeds intolerance, prejudice, and even fanaticism.

Not just educators have noticed social difficulties with home schoolers. One family doctor, Brian J. Penney, discovered in his practice that many home-schooled children "are ill equipped to deal with the real world. They often do not have the ability to cope with the distractions and peer pressures and thus may develop behaviour and attention problems." He also states that "home-schooled children do not appear to have developed the social maturity appropriate to their age" and are unable to perform well outside their home.

In response to such criticism, proponents of home schooling answer that home-schooled children have plenty of social opportunities. A study by Dr. Brian Ray of the National Home Education Research Institute found that an average home-schooled child participates in 5.2 activities per week outside the home. These children are involved in music, dance, drama, and art classes, visit museums and zoos, and join home-schooling groups or local churches. They form athletic teams and compete in home-school tournaments. They participate in book and foreign language clubs, scout groups, and have pen pals. Tracey and Thomas Sherry, home-schooling parents, believe these groups teach "positive social skills: kindness, patience, generosity, trust, empathy and cooperation."

In fact, home schoolers believe that, because the average time spent "in class" can often be compressed to about half a day, home-school students have more time available to them than do students in public school to pursue special interests. These activities may include practicing the piano, learning lines for a play, or studying ballet. One *60 Minutes* segment in 2001 spotlighted a family with five children, all of whom played piano and all of whom were accepted at the elite music academy Julliard—something that was unprecedented. As home-schooling students, they were able to practice many hours a day, something they would not have been able to do if they had attended public school.

Not only may home-schooled students have more time to focus on and nurture a talent, proponents of home schooling contend, they may also be able to choose more diverse experiences. The director of admissions for Marlboro College, Katherine Hallas, found that home-schooled applicants "have unique extracurricular backgrounds: One recent home-schooled applicant was the national quilting champion and another had traveled independently to Tibet to study shamanism."

Advocates of home schooling maintain that in the process of participating in outside activities, home-schooled children benefit by socializing with people of all ages, not just those of their peer group. They note that the world does not consist of people who are all the same age and that students are at a disadvantage if their day is spent only with peers. One home-schooling parent, William R. Mattox Jr., claims that home schooling "reduces that degree to which children find themselves constantly and obsessively being compared to, and comparing themselves with, other children their age." A home-schooled child's days, he believes, are more like the "real world" than that of students in public school.

Research conducted on the socialization of home-schooled children lends support to the arguments of home-schooling advocates. One study, according to Patricia Lines, found that home schoolers were as well-adjusted as public school students when measuring "aggression, reliance on others, perception of support from others, perceptions of limits to be followed, and interpersonal relations among family members." Another study indicated that home-schooled children had less behavioral problems than children attending public school.

Supporters of home schooling will often turn the tables on their critics, pointing to the negative influences present in public schools. In particular, a sizable percentage of home-schooling parents worry about the "wrong kind" of socialization found in public schools and keep their kids at home primarily for that reason. They believe the prevalence of illicit drugs, alcohol, smoking, and premarital sex undermines the moral principles taught at home. They fear the negative influences of peer pressure and want to protect their children from American pop culture.

Lastly, proponents of home schooling believe that the environment in a home-schooling household may be more conducive to participation in the community during adulthood. One 1996 study determined that parents who home school participate in civic activities more than parents with kids in public school. These civic activities included voting, attending public meeting or rallies, contributing to a political cause, or volunteering. Mattox comments that "homeschooled children tend to draw their primary social identity from their membership in a particular family rather than from their membership in a particular group," making them more likely to feel a part of the community.

Despite the fact that the debate about socialization persists, home schooling continues to thrive as an alternative educational choice. As of 1999, approximately 850,000 children were being home-schooled in the United States, growing at a rate of about 11 percent per year. The authors in *At Issue: Home Schooling* discuss the important issues surrounding the growth of home schooling and the role it will continue to play in American education.

1

Home Schooling Is Becoming More Common

Patricia M. Lines

Patricia M. Lines is a senior fellow at the Discovery Institute, an organization that publishes opinions on politics, technology, economics, science, and culture.

The home-schooling movement has expanded over the past fifteen years. Along with this expansion is an increased acceptance of home schooling as a legitimate form of education. In fact, home schooling has been around for centuries, while compulsory public schooling is a relatively new idea. The typical home-schooling parent is religious, white, and conservative, with a middle-class income and a better education level than most Americans. Home-schooling parents are more likely to participate in civic activities than parents who send their children to public school. Studies indicate that home-schooled children score above average on tests and are admitted by most universities and colleges in the United States.

The rise of homeschooling is one of the most significant social trends of the past half century. This reemergence of what is in fact an old practice has occurred for a distinctly modern reason: a desire to wrest control from the education bureaucrats and reestablish the family as central to a child's learning. Homeschooling is almost always a matter of choice. Schools are generally available, but homeschooling families have chosen not to use them.

The rapid growth of the homeschooling movement took the professional education establishment by surprise. When I estimated in 1985 that about 50,000 children were being homeschooled, one expert called it "wishful thinking, or at least artful advocacy." In 1990, as a researcher with the Department of Education, I suggested that the number had probably grown to 250,000 to 355,000 children. At the time, I based my estimate on three different sources: data from state education agencies; distribution of curricular packages for homeschoolers; and state homeschool

associations' estimates of their constituencies. As state data became more reliable, I turned to that source alone. The number continued to grow, and critics began citing my estimates.

The numbers are still growing. If states with reliable information are good indicators for the rest of the country, the number of homeschoolers nearly tripled in the five years from 1990–91 to 1995–96, when there were, according to the best possible estimate, about 700,000 homeschoolers. There is evidence, such as Florida's annual survey of homeschooling filers, that the population is growing at around 15 to 20 percent per year. I know of no state where the number is declining. It is extremely difficult to predict when the growth will taper off. If it keeps growing at this rate, there would be around 1.5 to 2 million children homeschooling by 2000–01 (about 3 to 4 percent of school-aged children nationwide). For a number of different reasons, parents are losing faith in the American classroom, and homeschooling is becoming a serious (and growing) alternative.

A haven from public school

Private schools have traditionally provided havens for those who dissent from the public school curriculum. Indeed, the competitive impact of homeschooling probably falls most heavily on private schools. Surveys suggest that among homeschooled children who previously attended a school, a disproportionate number attended a private school. A movement toward unstructured learning, strong and vigorous among some private schools in the 1960s, is now languishing, having lost many of its students to the liberal wing of the homeschooling movement and to various public school-choice programs. The Christian schools that sprung up in the 1980s have also lost students to homeschooling, but their growth curve was sufficiently strong that they remain robust. These schools also compete on a turf where public schools must not go—religious education. Still, when one might expect private schools to be growing, they are holding even. Homeschooling has taken up the slack.

In the broad sweep of time, universal, compulsory, and comprehensive schooling is a relatively new invention.

The contemporary homeschooling movement began sometime around mid century as a liberal, not a conservative, alternative to the public school. A handful of families (possibly as many as 10,000) in the late fifties and early sixties found schools too rigidly conservative. They pursued instead a liberal philosophy of education as advocated by educators such as the late John Holt, who believed that the best learning takes place without an established curriculum, and that the child should pursue his own interests with the support and encouragement of parents and other adults.

Then, in the 1980s, as the school culture drifted to the left, conservative and religious families were surprised to find themselves in a countercultural position. Many turned to Christian schools while others began homeschooling. Some believed religious duty required them to teach their own children; others sought to integrate religion, learning, and family life. Both the left and right wings of homeschooling are active today, and many families have both philosophical and religious reasons for their choice. Joining them are many homeschoolers who simply seek the highest quality education for their child, which they believe public and even private schools can no longer provide.

An old idea

Homeschooling is not a new idea or practice. For centuries children have learned outside formal school settings, even when schools were readily available. Thinkers from a variety of philosophical traditions have frowned upon formal schooling for a number of reasons. John Locke [17th-century English philosopher], for example, maintained that the primary aim of education was virtue, and that the home was the best place to teach it. Even John Dewey [American educator and philosopher] expressed regrets about formal schooling:

> A society is a number of people held together because they are working along common lines, in a common spirit, and with common aims. . . . The radical reason that the present school cannot organize itself as a natural social unit is because just this element of common and productive activity is absent.

Dewey held that school had been artificially "set apart" from society, and had become "so isolated from the ordinary conditions and motives of life" that it was "the one place in the world where it is most difficult to get experience—the mother of all discipline worth the name." He observed that "where the parent is intelligent enough to recognize what is best for the child, and is able to supply what is needed, we find the child learning." Dewey did not advocate homeschooling. He hoped instead to mimic the ideal home environment to create the ideal school. He thought teaching in the home could be done "only in a comparatively meager and haphazard manner." But given the choice between homeschooling and a rigid school system intent only on imparting information, Dewey might well have recommended homeschooling.

What is often forgotten is that in the broad sweep of time, universal, compulsory, and comprehensive schooling is a relatively new invention. Not until the nineteenth century did state legislatures begin requiring local governments to build schools and parents to enroll their children in them. Even then, compulsory requirements extended to only a few months a year. Not until the mid-twentieth century was universal high-school graduation a realistic goal. Even at this point, some traditional communities—such as the Seventh Day Adventists, Mormons, and Amish—continued to keep their school-aged children at home. Only recently have we begun to treat schooling as a full-time affair entrusted to professional teachers. And yet, in such a short span of time, most of the nation has come to accept classroom schooling as the norm, and so the recent upsurge in homeschooling has come to many as a surprise.

Three and four decades ago homeschooling was an unacceptable practice for satisfying compulsory education requirements in most states. The early pioneers of the contemporary movement often stayed "underground," and those who were discovered often faced fines or even jail. Gradually, state legislatures changed their laws, however, and all states now accept homeschooling as a legally valid alternative. Still, regulations vary from state to state. At a minimum, a family must file some basic information with either the state or local education agency. Some states have additional requirements, such as evaluation of homeschool students or minimal educational levels or testing for the homeschooling teacher. Many families still stay "underground"—out of fear that the legal environment will change again or because they disagree with particular regulations.

A homeschooling profile

The main difficulty in judging the scope of the homeschooling movement is limited and imperfect data. There is no definitive list of all homeschoolers in any locality, so the researcher usually must rely on a limited number of questions in a federally sponsored survey or on limited samples. If the latter, the sampled lists represent self-selected groups: members of a homeschooling association; those who file papers with the state in those states that require it; and subscribers to homeschooling magazines and newsletters. In addition, some homeschoolers refuse to respond to particular surveys: For example, a paranoid homeschooler may refuse to participate in a government survey while answering one from a homeschooling organization. Or a secular family that homeschools their children may not respond to a survey connected to, say, Bob Jones University [a Christian university]. To make matters even more difficult, a substantial and influential number of homeschoolers are philosophically opposed to cooperating with researchers.

With these cautions in mind, however, it is still possible to make some important observations about the movement. According to the surveys, the typical homeschooling family is religious, conservative, white, middle-income, and better educated than the general population. Homeschoolers are more likely to be part of a two-parent family, and there are usually two children of school age who are homeschooling and a third, usually younger child in the family. The mother typically assumes the largest share of the teaching responsibility, although fathers almost always pitch in, and in a substantial number of families—possibly as many as one out of ten—fathers take the primary responsibility. Despite this predominant profile, it is also clear that the full range of American families are trying or considering homeschooling.

Future growth could occur most rapidly among ethnic minorities. Though African Americans and other non-Caucasian groups are underrepresented among homeschoolers, the next generation of minorities is seriously considering it. In a survey of selected classes at Vanderbilt University and Nashville State Tech (a selective private university and a two-year college), almost half (45.3 percent) of the African-American students said "yes" or "maybe" when asked if they would homeschool their own children in the future. Among other non-Caucasian groups, two-thirds indicated "yes or "maybe." In contrast, less than one-fourth of the white students said this. The survey was small (254 students) and nonrandom, representing students enrolled in the classes of the researchers, whose influence was perhaps stronger among the non-Caucasian students. Nonetheless, the results are startling. Public educators who count on the loyalty of ethnic minorities as the backbone of their big-city clientele may be in for yet another surprise.

The curriculum

While both progressive and religious reasons for homeschooling remain important, a plurality of families say they are turning to homeschooling because they are dissatisfied with the quality of the public schools. Take, for example, a Florida Department of Education survey sent to homeschooling families for over a decade. Until 1994–95, the majority of families named "religion" as the reason why they chose homeschooling. This shifted in 1995 when, for the first time, the single most important reason for homeschooling became "dissatisfaction with the public school instructional program." Thirty-seven percent of parents gave this reason, compared to 29.6 percent who cited "Religious Reasons" that year. In 1995–96, the last year in which this survey question was asked, 42 percent of families cited dissatisfaction with the public school environment—especially safety, drugs, and adverse peer pressure. Religious reasons trailed at 27 percent, dissatisfaction with public school instruction at 16 percent, and other reasons at 15 percent.

A media stereotype would have homeschooling children start the day with a prayer and a salute to the flag and then gather around the kitchen table for structured lessons. This is . . . atypical.

A media stereotype would have homeschooling children start the day with a prayer and a salute to the flag and then gather around the kitchen table for structured lessons. This is not only atypical, it fails to present the full range of practices. Most homeschooling children spend time at libraries, museums, factories, nursing homes, churches, or classes offered at a local public school, a community college, a parks department, or elsewhere. Normally, parents plan and implement the learning program, although sometimes they find a tutor or older children organize their own independent study. It may be structured or unstructured; it may be affiliated with a public or private school; and it often involves shared lessons with other homeschooling families.

Critics of homeschooling sometimes highlight the lack of educational resources available to homeschoolers. But the resources can be found. Local support groups share experiences, meet for common activities, and help newcomers get started. Homeschooling associations provide advice and information, run conferences on legal, philosophical, and pedagogical issues, and review educational materials at exhibition booths. Electronic homeschool discussion groups abound. Parents also find guidance in books, magazines, and newsletters. Topics range from le-

gal issues to advice on learning disabilities and how to avoid burnout.

The resources also reflect the philosophical and pedagogical diversity of homeschoolers. The magazine *Drinking Gourd,* named after a folk song about the underground railway, provides articles and book reviews emphasizing cultural and ethnic diversity. *Nathan News,* published by the National Challenged Homeschoolers Associated Network, provides articles by parents and experts on such topics as "Auditory Memory Strategies and Activities," "Custom Fitting a Program for the LD [learning disabled] Child," or "My Recipe for IEP [Individualized Education Program]." In addition, parents obtain advice, texts, services, and curricula from public and private schools and other institutions. Alaska has served homeschooling students for decades through correspondence teaching. In California, a child may enroll in a public school independent-study program but base his studies in the home (the state does not like to call this "homeschooling"). Some states, such as Washington and Iowa, give families the right to enroll their children part-time in their local public schools and allow the district to claim a portion of the state's per pupil assistance for the enrollment. Some school districts sponsor centers where families may obtain resources, instructional support, and classes. Usually interested teachers or other public school professionals start these experimental partnerships. These programs are too new and varied to assess, but both teachers and parents who participate in them seem excited by the possibilities.

Report card

When people ask—How well do homeschoolers do?—they usually want to know about test scores. Of course, many homeschoolers reject this criterion, since their mission is to impart not simply skills but a particular set of values. That said, virtually all of the reported data show that homeschooled children score above average, sometimes well above average. Self-selection may affect this result, just as it affects other aspects of homeschooling research. Further, even where state law requires testing, substantial numbers of homeschoolers do not comply. Still, the available evidence suggests steady success. For example, Alaska, which has tested children in its homeschooling program for several decades, finds them, as a group, above average. In a very different study, commissioned by the Home School Legal Defense Association (HSLDA), a conservative Christian organization, Lawrence Rudner of the University of Maryland collected and analyzed results from the 12,000 students nationwide who had used the Bob Jones University testing services. The homeschooled children placed in the 62nd to 91st percentile of national norms, depending on the grade level and test subject area. Of course, we don't know how these same children would do in school. But there is certainly no evidence to suggest that homeschooling harms academic achievement.

Significantly, a handful of studies suggest that student achievement for homeschoolers has no relation to the educational attainment of the homeschooling parent. This is consistent with tutoring studies that indicate that the education level of a tutor has little to do with the achievement of a tutored child. One explanation might be that the advantages of one-to-one learning outweigh the advantages of professional training.

Homeschoolers have also had considerable success in college admissions. Karl M. Bunday, a homeschooler from Minnesota, maintains a web page that, at last check, lists over 900 colleges and universities that have admitted homeschoolers. Several years ago, I telephoned a small group of admissions officers to find out what they do with homeschoolers' applications. All (California Institute of Technology, Harvard-Radcliffe Colleges, Howard University, Stanford University, the University of Texas, and the University of Wisconsin) indicated that they are pleased to consider homeschooled teenagers for admission. All said that they would accept standardized admission test scores along with supportive material describing the subjects studied and other relevant experience. Some thought that well-qualified homeschoolers bring fresh diversity to their student body. Most admissions officers guessed that they had admitted as many as 1 percent of their undergraduates on this basis. Most also thought that some homeschoolers had slipped in unnoticed, submitting a high-school transcript obtained through a special program or a correspondence school.

The socialization factor

Critics often cite inadequate socialization as the fatal flaw in homeschooling. But such criticisms rest on certain professional assumptions about the nature of "healthy socialization." For the fact is that many homeschoolers worry about the values that predominate in the public school program and about negative peer pressure. They believe that it is preferable for children to spend more time with adults. But this does not mean that homeschooled children are isolated from their peers. They participate in homeschool support groups, scouting groups, churches, and other associations.

No one knows for certain what is the best kind of socialization; and there are important disagreements about what makes for a good and healthy child. Still, one can inquire, more narrowly and always imperfectly, about specific measurable elements of social development. For example, in one study of the social skills of homeschoolers and nonhomeschoolers, both groups scored as "well-adjusted," with comparable scores on scales measuring aggression, reliance on others, perception of support from others, perceptions of limits to be followed, and interpersonal relations among family members. Not surprisingly, the nonhomeschoolers scored somewhat higher in resolving interpersonal problems with other children. In another controlled study, a researcher videotaped 70 homeschooled children and 70 school children at play. Trained counselors viewed the videotapes and rated individual children without knowing the child's school status: They found the homeschooled children to have fewer behavioral problems. Of course, these kinds of studies are necessarily limited, but the findings provide no basis to question the social development of homeschooled children.

Public acceptance

All evidence suggests that homeschooling is here to stay, although it is hard to say when the growth will peak. Now that all states have adopted

flexible legislation and now that resources for homeschoolers are readily available, a significant factor contributing to growth will be public support. According to one survey, 95 percent of homeschoolers say they want or need "encouragement from family, friends, church, and community." In the 1980s, most Americans withheld support and encouragement. In 1985, only 16 percent of respondents to the annual Phi Delta Kappan Gallup poll thought that the homeschool movement was a "good thing"; 73 percent thought it was a "bad thing." By 1988, 28 percent rated it a good thing and 59 percent rated it a bad thing. By 1997, the approval rating had grown to 36 percent while the disapproval rating edged down to 57 percent.

In 1988, Gallup also asked whether parents should have a legal right to homeschool. A majority (53 percent) said they "should"; 39 percent said they "should not." When asked—"Do you think that the homeschools should or should not be required to meet the same teacher certification standards as the public schools?"—82 percent said "should" while only 12 percent said "should not." In 1997, the poll also asked whether "homeschools should or should not be required to guarantee a minimum level of educational quality"—88 percent responded affirmatively. The trend appears to be toward acceptance, so long as there is regulation.

But the most important factor in determining the future of homeschooling is the state of public and private schooling. In the nineteenth century, when public schools were Protestant in flavor, a vigorous Catholic school movement sprang up. Today, as the schools have become increasingly secular, a vigorous Christian (largely conservative Protestant) school movement developed. Today, both public and private schools operate like small bureaucracies, depending on professional expertise for most aspects of their program. As long as there are parents who object to the bureaucratic nature of today's schools, I would expect homeschooling to thrive.

Good citizens

Critics see homeschoolers as isolationist, atomistic, and even undemocratic. They think homeschooling violates the ideal of education as a public obligation—one that must be met, at least in part, through cooperative exchange within a community. But is this really an accurate picture of homeschooling? The hard evidence suggests that the vast majority of homeschooling families are more active in civic affairs than public school families.

Christian Smith and David Sikkink of the University of North Carolina found, based on responses to the 1996 National Household Education Survey, that homeschooling parents, along with other families who choose private schools, demonstrate higher levels of participation at almost every level of civic activity than do families who send their children to public schools. This included those choosing Catholic schools, other private religious schools, secular private schools, and homeschooling. Each of these groups were more likely to vote, contribute money to political causes, contact elected officials about their views, attend a public meeting or rally, or belong to community groups and volunteer associations. Smith and Sikkink found this to be true even after they compared only those families with similar education, income, age, race, family structure, region, and number of hours per week that parents worked. These characteristics explained some, but not all, of the higher civic and associational activity of the families who had chosen private schools or homeschooling.

American families from diverse backgrounds resort to homeschooling because they are dissatisfied with the philosophy, the content or the quality of American schools.

There is also plenty of anecdotal evidence that homeschoolers are interested in political efforts to reform education in general, and are especially interested in issues that affect homeschooling directly. Homeschoolers are capable of concerted political action. Several national and state organizations are capable of mobilizing large numbers of constituents wherever and whenever their interests are at stake. Probably the largest of these is HSLDA. Headed by Michael P. Farris, it employs a large legal staff specializing in homeschooling law. The organization routinely monitors developments in every state and keeps its membership informed of the legal limits on the authority of education officials. It is ready to negotiate or litigate where it believes its members' interests are threatened. An affiliated organization, the National Center for Home Education (NCHE), has a congressional-action program with a sophisticated electronic communication system. Other organizations, such as Clonlara Home Based Education (a secular institution located in Michigan and offering support to homeschoolers throughout the world), do the same for their constituencies. State associations are also active. As a result, efforts to pass stricter regulations or rules that threaten the authority of parents to homeschool their children are likely to face organized and informed opposition and sometimes lawsuits.

So far, homeschoolers have succeeded in winning a number of favorable policy changes—most notably, changes in state compulsory education laws. Homeschoolers have also flexed their political muscle in Congress. In 1994, Congressman George Miller offered a minor amendment to an omnibus education bill that, on one interpretation, would have required states to make sure all schools, including homeschools, had certified teachers. This was not explicit, and no one in Congress intended this. Worried nonetheless, HSLDA urged its membership to contact key Congressional offices, swamping targeted offices with mail and telephone calls. Representatives fell over each other to appease the homeschooling lobby. Congressmen Harold E. Ford, Jr., then chair of the education committee, and Dale E. Kildee offered an amendment that expressly excluded homeschooling from any provisions in the legislation. During floor debates, representatives praised homeschooling: One confessed that he was homeschooled as a child, and several proudly announced that their grandchildren were homeschooled. The Ford-Kildee amendment passed 424 to 1. Homeschoolers have also won federal legislation assuring equal treatment in access to federal loans and grants for postsecondary education.

The future

It is too early to tell whether homeschooling will establish itself as a major alternative to the modern school. But some things are clear: Homeschooling is becoming more common and more widely accepted. American families from diverse backgrounds resort to homeschooling because they are dissatisfied with the philosophy, the content, or the quality of American schools. The great majority of homeschooling families are not separatists and isolationists but active members of civil society. They seek to improve this nation, but they want to raise and educate their children in the meantime. Ultimately, they may help to inspire a great renewal of American education, or at least preserve values and ideas that are out of fashion within the education establishment.

2

Home Schooling Is Increasing Among African Americans

Sandy Coleman

Sandy Coleman is a staff writer for the Boston Globe.

More African Americans and other minorities are choosing to home school their children for academic and cultural reasons. Internet resources make home schooling more affordable today, and African American home-school support groups are emerging. While there are challenges for these families, they value the opportunities to discuss race issues with their children. Some African American educators criticize the African American flight from public schools after the right to an equal education was so hard fought. However, studies show there is less academic disparity between Caucasians and African Americans in home-schooling environments than in public schools.

When naming their three black boys, Michelle and Alan Shaw chose words that would underscore treasured roots and religion: Chinua, Nigerian for God's own blessing; Yesuto, Ghanaian for belongs to Jesus; and Obasi, Nigerian for in honor of God.

So, when it came to selecting the best school for their boys, the Dorchester couple—she an attorney with a Harvard law degree, he a computer expert with a master's degree and doctorate from MIT—took the same care.

Home, they decided, was the best place to teach their children strong academics, religious values, and instill their own sense of ethnic pride.

"For black people in this country, there is a need for not letting our kids forget their history," said Alan Shaw, whose sons are 3, 6, and 7. "We shouldn't look to something that's been designed by the state as a way for us to teach our kids about their past and their future."

Fueled by a desire to rescue their children from academic failure and neglect at the hands of overburdened public schools and determined to weave tight-knit families, more African-Americans and other minorities nationwide are deciding that when it comes to school, there's no place like home.

This, even as they are accused of abandoning the very public school system that for decades minorities who fought to overcome separate and unequal education have been told is the ticket up and out of oppression.

"Many of them have recognized that academically the public school system has not saved them," said Brian Ray, president of the National Home Education Research Institute, a nonprofit based in Oregon.

A growing diversity

While there are no concrete figures, anecdotally, specialists say there is a growing diversity in home schooling. Single parents are venturing into it, and it is proving to be a sanctuary for many interracial couples. In the past, homeschooling has been a choice made mostly by white, middle-income families who could afford setting themselves apart from the traditional educational system.

"Homeschooling has now become so prevalent that it has gotten to the point where it is not seen as wacky or nutty," Ray said. "So it makes it easier for minorities to try it."

He estimates that there are about 1.3 million to 1.7 million K–12 homeschooled children nationwide, about 1 percent of those black and a lesser percentage Hispanic. "I think over the next five years, you're going to see real growth," he said.

The rapid expansion and growth in use of the Internet also has meant plenty of inexpensive resources for homeschoolers, easing some socioeconomic barriers. A book written in 1996, *Freedom Challenge: African American Homeschoolers,* even features essays by 15 families that serve as a road map.

The interest in homeschooling is growing so much that Joyce and Eric Burges of Baker, La., are creating a national networking group that encourages African-Americans to homeschool.

"My husband and I want to put a beacon of light out there that says this is an option, this is a choice you have," said Joyce Burges, an executive secretary who homeschools three children. Missy and Rick Parker, who have been homeschooling for 16 years, created a similar group in 1994 in Detroit.

"It's a matter of commitment," said Missy Parker, a Southern Baptist who homeschools to teach religious values. She estimates that at least 200 African-American families in Detroit are homeschooling. "Most African-Americans wouldn't venture to do it because they didn't feel they were equipped. But, that's what the support group is for, so you don't have to do it on your own."

The criticisms

Homeschooling, however, doesn't come without challenges or criticisms as any family, black or white, knows. These include fear of the unknown, lack of support from relatives and friends, financial belt-tightening and questions about the legitimacy of homeschooling.

And for African-Americans the accusation of black flight.

"Anything that we take away from the public schools, especially in the cities has a detrimental effect," said Steven C. Leonard, headmaster of the Jeremiah E. Burke High School in Dorchester. "I would much rather have minority parents, black parents, all parents, fight to strengthen the public school systems because like it or not that's where the bulk of the students who compose our future will be educated."

Other African-American educators believe students lose something when parents chose to school at home.

"One of the great benefits of public schooling is that we teach people, children, how to both ask for help from others as well as to give help to others who need it," said Charles Willie, a Harvard professor emeritus and one of the designers of Boston public school's controlled-choice assignment plan. "These are valuable learnings that are difficult to replace in an isolated learning environment."

The education disparity

Still, minorities are choosing to homeschool for reasons as diverse as the ways in which they are teaching their children.

Some, like the Shaws, say the public school system is failing African-American children, who often end up at the bottom of achievement assessments. Results by race on the 1999 Massachusetts Comprehensive Assessment System showed black and Latino students behind whites in every category for every grade.

Home . . . was the best place to teach their children strong academics, religious values, and instill their own sense of ethnic pride.

In contrast, the Shaws point to a 1997 study by Ray and the Home School Legal Defense Association showing less of a disparity between achievement rates in math and reading among minority and white homeschoolers.

In addition, lamenting the loss of close-knit black communities, some parents say homeschooling allows them to fortify their children in nuturing environments.

"This early stage is critical to establishing what is important, what we believe in," said Alan Shaw, a computer consultant who works from home.

Cases of public school neglect

Some, like Kevin Brooks, a divorced father in Arlington, say they are homeschooling to compensate for school systems that allow too many children to fall through the cracks.

Brooks, a researcher for Motorola, pulled his 14-year-old son Kristoff out of public school in February when he found he was spending hours trying to help his son through course work the youth should have already mastered. This year, Brooks also plans to home school Kristoff's twin sister.

He uses a network of friends, black and white, to help teach Kristoff. "One of my challenges, and it will increase, is feeling comfortable having someone who isn't black talk to my kids about issues of race one-on-one," said Brooks, who shares custody with his former wife.

During a recent homeschooling session, one of Brooks' white friends and Kristoff had a complex conversation on how black people are sometimes portrayed negatively in cartoons. It taught Brooks a lesson: "When you are learning from the world, outside the classroom system, you are exposed to more things," he said. "So talking about stuff is a lot more important now."

From the moment that Beverley Foreman, a Jamaica native, set foot in this country in 1976, she had trouble with traditional schools. It started with her youngest son, who at 5 was already at a second-grade level, able to read and write in cursive. Here, he was placed in kindergarten and put in a corner to play with blocks, she said.

"He became so distracted and disinterested in school," she said, and watched as he was bused out of his community to a school with special needs students, and told her son might have attention deficit disorder.

He eventually graduated from high school, but after that Foreman pulled her other children out of public schools. The Maynard mother of four boys was "terrified" when she began homeschooling seven years ago, but she got over her fear and is still homeschooling her youngest son using libraries and museums as classrooms.

It is worth it

The teachable moments, insist the families, prove it is worth it over and over again. The Shaws, for example, were there when one son assumed God was white. They told him God has no color but people generally project on Him an image with which they identify.

And while it was their parents' choice, some minority homeschool children also applaud the move.

Candace Burges, 15, values the one-on-one attention. "If I were in school now, the average teacher has to teach about 30 kids in one classroom. With my room, it's only three," she said.

And self-esteem, Burges said, is nurtured at home. "Sometimes African-American students are underestimated in school and they are teased and people really don't know who they really are," she said.

Alan Shaw, who attended public schools, says he never envisioned homeschooling his children. But, back in college he was one to go against the grain, he said.

"I've always been hoping there would be some alternative to mainstream life," Shaw said. He found it at home.

The Challenges of Home Schooling

Debra Bell

Debra Bell is founder of the online Home School Resource Center and the Young Writer's Institute. She teaches English at the Creative Home Educators Support Services and is the author of The Ultimate Guide to Homeschooling, *from which the following viewpoint was taken.*

Home schooling as a way of life demands a lot of preparation and instruction time. While parents' expectations may be high, they should keep in mind that every home-school environment will have strengths and weaknesses and that home schooling will not cure family problems. Although every child benefits from one-on-one instruction, a parent's educational background may be a limitation while home schooling. Also, a child may lack the motivation that is often generated by competition in a public setting. Exclusion from scholastic sports can also decrease opportunities for healthy competition. Lastly, a lack of oversight over home schoolers can result in inadequate education.

When I was nine I got braces. The dental assistant who put the plaster of Paris in my mouth to make the mold said, "This is going to taste great, just like oatmeal." Well, I loved oatmeal as a kid, and I eagerly bit down on the mash she had scooped into my mouth. To this day I remember my disillusionment and astonishment that she had lied to me. (I believe that woman later wrote the book *Childbirth Without Pain.*)

And that is why I'm going to tell you the downside of homeschooling. I don't want any angry letters accusing me of an inflated sales pitch.

If you don't take the time to sit down and count the cost, as well as to lay a solid foundation in the grace of God before you begin to homeschool, you'll spend much of your time dealing with double-mindedness instead of seizing the opportunity at hand.

Frustration, discouragement, ambivalence: These are common emotions you will live with if you choose to homeschool. My friend Peggy calls homeschooling "the crucible of my life." It not only constantly

From *The Ultimate Guide to Homeschooling*, by Debra Bell (Cheltenham, England: Thomas Nelson, Inc., 1997). Copyright © 1997 by Debra Bell. Reprinted with permission of the publisher.

brings to the surface her children's character flaws but her own as well. And she can't put off dealing with them.

It's very common for the conversations in the mothers' lounge at the Learning Center homeschool co-op to center around the challenges and discouragement of homeschooling. Not only do our children need these bimonthly group experiences, but we moms need the support and reenvisioning that comes from upholding one another.

Some of the difficulties I want to address can be minimized. . . . But others are inherent in the choice and must be weighed before you decide.

Time demands

No matter how you approach it, homeschooling is a tremendous investment of time and energy. It's not another interest to fit into an already busy schedule. It's a way of life.

Other family members may have needs that require a competing time commitment. Perhaps you are caring for an elderly parent or a child with special needs. Perhaps you are working and do not have the option of quitting or scaling back your hours. In these situations, you may not have the time to give that homeschooling requires.

My friend Barb is deeply committed to the principles of homeschooling. However, her third child, Anna, has had some learning delays, and she needs a lot of one-on-one attention in order to move forward. The time Barb was investing in Anna was leaving her older children without enough direction. After a particularly dissatisfying homeschooling year (when her oldest son, Adam, had most of his schoolwork "artistically" rearranged by Anna), Barb and her husband, Steve, reluctantly visited a publicly funded intermediate unit classroom that serves their public school district—and were pleasantly surprised. The teacher was supportive of Barb's commitment to homeschooling, and Barb continues to work with Anna at home, but having Anna also enrolled several days a week in this therapy program has given Barb the time she needs for her other kids as well.

On the other hand, another friend with a special-needs child chose in the end to enroll her two older children in school as part of the solution to the time commitment her youngest daughter needs.

Even without extenuating circumstances, homeschooling is, in the end, primarily a time commitment. The time you might have given to a career or ministry gets diverted here. For women who have worked solely at home or who have children that have not yet been to school, the transition to homeschooling is usually not as big an adjustment as it is for the woman who must leave the work force or pull her children out of a traditional setting. If you are in the latter situation, then you need to be realistic about the adjustment and sense of restraint the transition to homeschooling will bring into your life.

Preparation time

While the actual time devoted to homeschooling your kids is far less than the time they would spend in school each day, you still have lots of things to do to prepare for that instructional time. To maximize the opportunities homeschooling affords, you need to be self-educating and constantly fine-tuning your program. . . . Kids can't teach themselves. You need to provide daily accountability, direction and tutoring.

My first year as a classroom teacher was very difficult because I had to create the courses I was teaching. But the years following were much less time consuming because I often taught the same courses over again. That's not true in homeschooling. Every year there's a different schedule. Every year there's new coursework to oversee. And even though Katie and Kristen are following behind the boys, in tailoring the program to their needs and interests, I'm doing a lot of new things with them as well.

The need for private time

Depending upon our temperaments, never having a break from the kids or time to ourselves can be a difficult demand. I don't think homeschooling needs to be as restrictive as many people imagine in order to succeed. But the amount of time you can carve away from your responsibilities is certainly limited, and we have to be creative about finding moments of relaxation.

Once I spent a few days with a college roommate whose two children were doing well in public school. She hadn't yet returned to the work force, and her weekly schedule included aerobic classes, women's Bible study, and lunch with friends. Her house was neat as a pin and beautifully decorated. I returned home grumpy and envious.

Frustration, discouragement, ambivalence: These are common emotions you will live with if you choose to homeschool.

I find I need to keep blinders on to maintain my contentment in homeschooling. Now that my children are older, I really do enjoy their company and don't think much about the limits of my life. But when they were little, it didn't come quite so naturally—by a long shot. I needed to stay fixed on the conviction that this was God's will for my life and He had designed the limits of my freedom, not just for my children's good, but for my own good as well. I can't let myself look at the "freedom" I think other women have and get resentful. But it's not always easy.

Before you choose to homeschool, answer these questions:
- Am I able and willing to devote the time necessary to do this right?
- Will I have enthusiasm for teaching my children and be dedicated to seeking out opportunities and strategies for maximizing this opportunity?

If your answer is no, your children will probably be better served in a classroom setting with a teacher who is enthused about teaching and creative in his or her approach.

Many parents who want the benefits of an environment that reflects their value system but can't give the time necessary to teach the academics invest their energy in setting up a private school for their kids; classical schools, charter schools, parent-run schools, and hybrids of private and homeschooling like Creative Home Educators' Support Services (CHESS) are springing up all over the country. And in many places, it's still possible for parents to have a positive impact on their public schools through involvement in parent organizations, or booster clubs or by serving on their school board.

Unrealistic expectations

When we make the choice to homeschool, it's with the expectation of results commensurate with the sacrifices we are about to make. Or at the very least, we want enough evidence to prove our skeptics wrong. And we want it soon.

Many of us enter homeschooling anticipating immediate success. A spouse or relative may be adding pressure to that anticipation as well. With the prevalent hard sell of homeschooling and with all the glowing reports of individual students' successes, it's very easy to set unrealistic expectations for ourselves and for our children.

Another frequent assumption is that homeschooling will remove our children's character flaws, rescue them from academic failure, or miraculously cure family problems.

I think the homeschool moms of the Learning Center homeschool co-op I direct are the absolute cream of the crop. They are creative, diligent, and fervent in their faith. As we gathered to open our school year with prayer, I was surprised to hear how discouraged and wrought with guilt most of the moms were. They were very conscious of all they were not getting done in their homes and homeschools. They were worried that they were not doing something right with one or more of their kids. And they were sure they were the only one failing in this way. By the time it was my turn to share, I was feeling very guilty about not feeling guilty! And by golly, I then found it easy to make a list of all I was falling short on as well.

From my travels I've heard the same angst in many, many mothers' voices.

Homeschooling has trade-offs

Homeschooling is a trade-off. There are always going to be things that are not done or not done well. Howard Richman, a homeschool evaluator and researcher in Pennsylvania, evaluates more than five hundred home-schooled children every year. His cumulative research is very impressive. High SAT scores, high achievement scores, post-graduate success. But in his analysis of individual homeschool programs, what he consistently sees are strengths and weaknesses in every home. We do some things very well (usually homeschoolers raise very literate kids), but we sacrifice time in other areas to do so (say, in my case, science).

I minimize the impact of my weaknesses by involving my children in many cooperative learning experiences where they have other teachers who offset my shortcomings. But time restraints still prevent us from doing everything as well as I can envision. I have to be at peace with the gap between the ideal and the reality.

Homeschooling is not a cure-all

Another frequent assumption is that homeschooling will remove our children's character flaws, rescue them from academic failure, or miraculously cure family problems. But the converse is true: Homeschooling will exacerbate these situations. These issues typically must be addressed at a more fundamental level. Homeschooling is an educational choice, not a biblical solution for fractures in our family life. . . .

I ask you to evaluate the health of your family relationships before beginning to homeschool. It's important that you have a realistic picture here and that you have a plan for dealing with these weaknesses if you want to minimize, not maximize, the stress homeschooling can bring.

I have seen numerous families undertake homeschooling as a last-ditch effort to prevent a rebellious teenager from dropping out of school. Unfortunately the issues that led to this impasse sprouted long ago. Homeschooling may be a good option for cutting off negative influences aggravating the situation, but "tough love" and biblical counseling are more likely to make the real difference in this child's life.

When you consider homeschooling, you must recognize that the fruit you hope to realize will likely take longer and be harder to grow than you anticipate. In many cases you must merely live in faith for the future results. I watched Cindy spend most of her homeschooling years with Nate, her oldest, very ambivalent about the choice she had made. Then, shortly after his freshman year of college, Nate told his parents how grateful he was to have been homeschooled and how well prepared he felt he had been for college life. It's hard to quantify how much his comments meant to Cindy or how challenging the wait had been to hear them.

The limits on community involvement

Homeschooling can limit your family's impact and outreach in your community. School forms a natural vehicle for getting to know other families and opening opportunities to share our faith and lives. Christian teachers, students, and parents whose character squares with the values they espouse can make a real difference in other children's lives and better their schools and community through their service.

For ten years, Kermit and I served on the board of a pregnancy care center we founded. Today this center operates three offices and reaches more than a thousand women annually. We loved being a part of a ministry that's making a tangible difference, coupling the gospel with meeting legitimate needs in our community. And we loved the people we labored with. Stepping down from active involvement there was one of the most difficult decision I've had to make. But it was necessary if I was going to homeschool my children with integrity.

The center has likewise lost many volunteers because they have chosen to homeschool their children. It has created a dilemma that has been difficult to resolve.

Churches can feel this same tension. Many needs that were once met by the women of the church now go unmet because moms are reentering the workforce or homeschooling.

It's become a sore point in the church. It's a challenge to not become critical of the homeschool movement when the obvious impact these strong Christian families could be having is shifted away from legitimate needs.

This is a drawback I believe can be minimized. Many homeschool families I know with older children have found ways to reach out to others as part of their homeschool programs. The flexibility that homeschooling affords makes short-term missions trips a real possibility. Our co-op has done a number of service projects and put on an after-school program at the city mission. It's not always easy to facilitate these opportunities, but homeschool families who make outreach a priority find creative ways to serve in their churches and communities.

Teacher limitations

It's hard to beat the one-on-one instruction homeschooling can provide for a child. But even with all its benefits, I find there are some drawbacks for our children that need to be considered, especially as they grow older.

Our children will benefit from our strengths and be limited by our weaknesses if we do not offset them. My kids are fluid writers. Gabe has been published and paid twice. In fifth grade he and Mike generated more than twenty thousand original words for school assignments. Katie routinely writes ten-page stories. They all read avidly and wish they were getting speaking engagements instead of their mother. Obviously they've benefited from the strength of my background. But they've suffered for my limits as well.

Katie attended her first Young Writers' Institute with Sigmund Brouwer in third grade. I was watching the children complete an assignment for Sigmund when I noticed all the other children (thirty-four of them to be exact) were composing their stories in cursive. Katie was laboriously printing hers. I suddenly realized I had completely forgotten to teach my daughter cursive handwriting! It just never entered my brain. I was almost hyperventilating over the panic attack that ensued—if I could forget cursive, what other venal or mortal oversight was I capable of? Would my daughter ever recover? What doors were now swinging shut because of her mother's incompetency?

Real change or progress in life is difficult to bring about without some level of accountability.

Of course I overreacted, and Katie survived. Handwriting isn't a life-and-death skill, but this experience illustrated for me the impact the limits of my abilities or initiative can have on my children.

I disagree with homeschooling families that isolate their kids. It's not healthy, and the children will not have the opportunity to hone their skills and character as they rub shoulders with others with different strengths and weaknesses.

A church is not healthy without every member contributing his or her gifts and talents to church life. A homeschool isn't healthy either if we misconstrue Scripture to mean parents are to be the *only* influence or teachers in our children's lives.

It is so important that we recognize our limitations and seek out opportunities for our kids to offset those limitations.

Lack of recognition

Many of the homeschooled kids I've evaluated have had tremendous academic and artistic achievements—but often these accomplishments are unrecognized. While the local papers feature pictures of school happenings and recognition of individual students, the homeschool community is mostly overlooked.

Several of the homeschooled students I've worked with have now transitioned into a public high school and have done exceptionally well. It is gratifying for me to see all the awards they've garnered. Frankly, they've found the accolades pretty motivational, too.

Appropriate recognition is an important source of motivation for adults and children. And local homeschool communities are beginning to find creative ways to recognize the accomplishments of students—awards banquets, exhibits at conventions, juried science and history fairs, graduation ceremonies. I'd like to see us go further by inviting the local media to these events. The local newspaper is not purposefully overlooking the homeschooled kids; it just doesn't have a clue as to what we are doing. It's our job to educate them.

The benefits of competition

I've changed my views on competition over the years, and it's come from observing my identical twin sons. I've had to conclude that the natural competitiveness between them has been to their benefit.

When the first one began to read, the other was motivated to work harder at his own reading. When Michael works ahead in algebra, Gabe complains but buckles down and catches up. When one can beat the other racing or throwing a ball, the other works harder to exceed the standard. Once he does, then his brother stretches himself even further to surpass his twin's accomplishments once again.

Now, before you imagine a cutthroat environment at our house, let me assure you they haven't risked their relationship over this. They are best friends and have agreed on their own never to compete against each other publicly. (For example, rather than wrestle each other in a tournament, they ask the referee to flip a coin to determine the winner.)

Competition can be an important motivational tool, especially for older students. I've worked with quite a few families who found that a traditional setting was better suited for their teenagers (usually boys) because they needed an element of competition to be motivated to learn.

The CHESS classes Cindy McKeown has organized have demonstrated to me the benefits of competition in a carefully controlled environment. In this setting, the kids admire the students who do their best. My three oldest kids invest a lot more time on assignments for their classes there than on assignments they do at home because they know their projects are going to be displayed alongside those produced by their peers. They don't want to be embarrassed.

Accountability is needed for discipline

I've edited this section out of [my viewpoint] several times because I know I am going to take flak for it from my good friends who believe the state usurps parental authority when it requires any level of accountability from homeschoolers. Philosophically, I don't disagree with those who dislike this government oversight, but I am also a pragmatist.

In many places it is easy to home-educate without much outside accountability or government regulations. I'm not advocating tougher laws, but I do see a drawback that can work against our children's best interests if we allow it to.

Real change or progress in life is difficult to bring about without some level of accountability. That's why the Bible says, "confess your sins to one another" (James 5:16), and it's why accountability groups like Weight Watchers and Alcoholics Anonymous work.

At least in my own life, where I lack accountability I typically lack discipline. I do a much better job homeschooling my children now than I did prior to the enactment of our state law that requires an annual review of our program. I have gained valuable insights from my evaluator (chosen by my husband and me, not by the state), and my kids really look forward to sharing their schoolwork each June with her. The families I evaluate have often commented on the helpfulness of an outside review as well.

Without some kind of accountability, it is easy to slide year after year toward an undisciplined lifestyle. Are our kids learning to meet deadlines and to complete a course of study, sticking to it even when they are tired or disinterested in the material? A traditional setting does provide this framework. I personally find that framework too restrictive, but some framework is still beneficial.

If you home-educate in a state where little accountability is required, consider building accountability into your program. Deadlines, goals for the year in the core subject areas, and an annual day of sharing your work with others in your homeschool support group (especially for your older students) can *only* improve your program. We want our kids to cultivate a disciplined lifestyle, and that doesn't come from only doing those things they feel like doing.

Exclusion from scholastic sports

Almost any opportunity available to conventionally schooled students is now open to kids who are homeschooled—except for scholastic sports. Academic competitions, such as *Knowledge Open, Global Challenge, Math-Counts*, and *Odyssey of the Mind*, have adjusted their requirements to accept homeschoolers. Extracurricular activities in music, drama, dance, etc., can all be found at a competitive level outside of your local school district. But the athletic competition that will open doors to college-level play or scholarships often is not. And this has been a frequent reason for homeschooled students to enroll in a traditional setting.

For some of you a passionate devotion to competitive sports is hard to comprehend. Kermit and I did not set out to raise athlete. It doesn't rank high on our list of targets in and of itself. We saw our recreation league's sports program as an arena for integrating our lives with those in our community. So we innocently signed our sons up for T-ball when they were five. One thing led to another, and before I knew it I'd spent equivalent to a year of my life watching Mike and Gabe play baseball and my daughters play softball—and that's just the summer.

My children play competitive sports year-round—we have training videos, they go to camps, and we have a room-size wrestling mat in our basement and a mini weightroom. We have a shelf lined with athletic trophies and only two scrawny academic ones—though they are front and center. It's completely out of balance, and I can't think of anything I get more pleasure from than watching my kids and their friends play (and win!) competitively.

To say I was worried about what we were going to do when my sons no longer had access to competitive sports is an understatement. We've played on homeschool volleyball teams and basketball teams. Those are pretty easy to pull together, but Mike and Gabe wrestle and play football. I like a challenge, but there is no way I'm going to pull together a home-schooled wrestling team and then find a league to play in, at least not in this century.

So, two years before their teams were scheduled to come under the jurisdiction of the school district, I started a dialogue with my school board. In the end they extended to the homeschool community not only access to sports but also access to all extracurricular activities and secondary classes.

This is currently an issue heating up in the homeschool community. Several states have already legislated access to scholastic sports for homeschoolers, and around the country many homeschool families have a cooperative relationship with their school district. But those open doors have all come about through hard work.

And in most places the doors remain closed.

4

Home Schooling Is a Legitimate Alternative to Public Schools

Chris Jeub

Chris Jeub is assistant editor of Focus on the Family's LifeWise *magazine, a Christian publication for readers over fifty. He also edits the* Christian Debater, *a newsletter for debaters, and is president of the Training Minds Ministry.*

Parents who home school have been criticized by the educational community for choosing to teach their children outside the public school setting. Despite such criticism, a growing number of parents opt to home school for varied reasons. One reason is that home-schooled students can participate in clubs and support groups without being exposed to drugs, sex, or violence. Another reason is that the academic freedom afforded by home schooling allows for one-on-one instruction and presents opportunities for student creativity and independent thinking. Additionally, religious education can be included as part of the child's curriculum. For these reasons, home schooling succeeds in passing down America's cultural heritage, which is the true purpose of education.

Home schooling neither isolates children nor harms their academic growth; it does, however, come close to the true definition of education: the passing down of culture.

"So, where do your children go to school?"

Of all the casual questions one teacher could ask another, this one always puts butterflies in my stomach.

"Well, uh, my wife and I tutor them," I say. Then I try to change the subject—but never quickly enough.

"Tutored?" they say, squinting their nose and ruffling their brows "You mean home schooled?"

These situations never fail to begin an hour-long discussion on why we home school our children. This should not surprise me, though.

From "Why Parents Choose Home Schooling," by Chris Jeub, *Education Leadership*, September 1994. Copyright © 1994 by the Association for Supervision and Curriculum Development.

Home schooling is unusual and a bit radical. It is natural for educators—or anyone for that matter—to question a practice that is so lightly researched.

Ten years ago there were roughly 15,000 home schools nationally; today, according to the U.S. Department of Education, there are 350,000. Hundreds of national magazines and newspapers, numerous home-school curriculum distributors, and countless numbers of networks and contact groups address home-school issues.

As a public school teacher myself, I asked many questions and read much before I decided to school my children at home. And I believe that choice has been the best decision I have made for their education.

True social development takes place in the home, not in the schools.

Lately, many in the educational community have attacked the home-school community with little regard for the harm they do to families and the education of children. For example, a proposed federal bill required all school teachers—home-school and private school teachers, too—to be certified in every disciplinary area. Under this bill, even though I have a diploma and certificate to teach secondary English, I would not be able to teach my grade-school children. If it hadn't been for the quick and loud uprising of America's home schoolers, this bill would have passed and home schooling would be illegal.

Generally, parents choose to home school their children for social, academic, family, and/or religious reasons. As for me, many educators are surprised to hear that academic reasons influenced me most.

Social reasons

In public schools, socialization techniques, such as classroom management, peer grouping, and extracurricular activities, take much time and effort. But must children learn such basic life skills as working together, sharing, and showing respect for others through formalized classroom experiences? Critics charge that home-schooled children will be socially handicapped and unable to adapt to real-life interaction when older; the fact is, however, that these children have many opportunities to interact with peers. In *Growing Without Schooling*, Pat Farenga writes:

> Certainly group experiences are a big part of education, and home schoolers have plenty of them. Home schoolers write to us about how they form or join writing clubs, book discussion groups, and local home-schooling support groups. Home schoolers also take part in school sports teams and music groups, as well as the many public and private group activities our communities provide. . . . Home schoolers can and do experience other people and cultures without going to school.

Of course, not all socialization is good for a child. For example, some social activity leads to experiences with drugs, alcohol, tobacco, harassment, premarital sex, guns, and violence. The positive side of socialization—sharing respect, communication, getting along, and relating to others—can be wonderfully fulfilled in a home-school setting. As Raymond S. Moore, a leader in the home-school movement, says:

> Parents and educators usually talk about sociability, but neglect to differentiate the kind of sociability they prefer. The child who feels needed, wanted, and depended on at home, sharing responsibilities and chores, is much more likely to develop a sense of self-worth and a stable value system—which is the basic ingredient for a positive sociability. In contrast is the negative sociability that develops when a child surrenders to his peers.

Those who believe in the home-school philosophy also think that six to eight hours of extra social and community activities after school and weekends is a bit much. Science says it's a bit much, too. Behavioral psychologist Urie Bronfenbrenner concluded that "meaningful human contact" is best accomplished in environments where few people are around. Any teacher will agree that the smaller the class size, the more learning takes place. In a survey concerning positive self-concept, John Wesley Taylor found that half of 224 home-schooled children scored above the 90th percentile, and only 10 percent were below the national average. True social development takes place in the home, not in the schools.

Academic reasons

Shouldn't educational experts be trusted with the academic training of our students? How is it possible for parents—especially parents with little or no postsecondary education—to teach children every discipline? Even with my bachelor of science degree in English, how can I be qualified to teach math or science to my 2nd and 4th grade children?

If these assumptions were true, home-school kids would not be some of the most successful people in society. William Blake, Charles Dickens, Agatha Christie, Benjamin Franklin, Woodrow Wilson, Winston Churchill, Florence Nightingale, Charlie Chaplin, the Wright Brothers, Thomas Edison, and Andrew Carnegie were all famous home-schooled students.

Students have both the freedom to pursue their natural desires and the attention needed to develop ways of thinking that come more difficult to them.

The assumption that home-school parents are not expert enough to teach is based on a faulty definition of education. Education is not necessarily teaching what the teacher knows, or training students in a particular skill. Separating disciplines from other disciplines—as if English had nothing to do with math, and science had nothing to do with civics—is grossly misrepresenting what education really is: the passing on of a culture.

A wise saying goes: "A good teacher teaches himself out of a job." When I teach English, I am not merely teaching my students what I learned in college. I am teaching children to love literature and to passionately engage in the language arts. I integrate all disciplines—history, science, social studies, math—into my lessons. Real life is interdisciplinary; to teach otherwise would not be teaching our culture.

Few professionals would disagree that one-to-one tutoring creates an atmosphere that is healthy, productive, and conducive to a student's academic success. That's why I often say I tutor my children, rather than home school them.

Educational philosophy today supports the concept that education is more than rote learning. For example, outcome-based education recognizes that students need to develop at their own pace, whole language integrates all disciplines, and modern Montessori methods emphasize the need for individual attention and assessment. Home schooling accomplishes all of these. Students have both the freedom to pursue their natural desires and the attention needed to develop the ways of thinking that come more difficult to them. Pat Farenga says, "Children, like adults, need time to be alone to think, to muse, to read freely, to daydream, to be creative, to form a self independent of the barrage of mass culture." While granting students this time in traditional schools has always been a struggle, that is not true of home schools.

Family reasons

Critics of home schools claim that we shelter our children from the real world. Home-school parents sometimes accuse public schools of stealing children from the home and their parents. Neither is a mature argument, and neither is true.

No other factor in life, however, will have more of an impact on a child than family background. Every teacher knows that a student having problems at home most likely will not produce in class and that students with wholesome, functional families are usually the exceptional students. Home-school parents see the family as superior to any other institution in society. When the educational institution threatens the family, these parents tend to choose to educate their children at home.

To say public schools undermine the family is just as alarmist as saying home schools will ruin the education of our children. Yet, many in education today devalue the importance of the family. Schools have redefined family values and, in some cases, ridiculed the cultural beliefs of the students and their parents. For example, many home-school parents choose to take their children out of school because of the school's teachings on sensitive issues like premarital sex, same-sex relationships, questioning of authority, and secular religion.

Religious reasons

Religion is a major part of the American culture, but public schools fail to take religion seriously. Fear of church and state laws keep schools from even mentioning the influence of religion in American life. History and civics textbooks never mention the religious faiths of important leaders.

Martin Luther King Jr. is rarely named with his title of reverend. That John F. Kennedy was the first Catholic president, Albert Einstein was a Jew, and the Abolitionists were led by evangelical Christians are facts ignored. And textbooks rarely describe the influence that religion may have had on these great achievers.

Instead of working side-by-side with the religious establishment, the educational establishment has attempted to strangle religion's influence. Instead of recognizing religion as part of our culture, many have fought hard in the courts to make religion illegal in the classroom.

Everyone recognizes that public schooling has it place. Home schooling, too, is a healthy educational choice. Parents who have the dedication to do it should have every right to choose it.

5

Public School Is a
Better Choice than
Home Schooling

Evie Hudak

Evie Hudak serves on the Colorado PTA Board of Directors. She has also worked on the Steering Committee of the Colorado Education Network and on the State Accountability Committee and is a member of the Coalition for a Higher Performance Education System and the National Association of State Boards of Education.

Public schools offer students a safe learning environment, social interaction, highly qualified instructors, and a system of accountability, making them the best place for a child's education. Input from parents, teachers, and administrators infuse public schools with new ideas. These individuals are committed to instilling in students the fundamental values that make democracy possible. On the other hand, parents who are home schooling their children must meet no requirements in terms of training or certification and are not evaluated. Moreover, home-schooled students do not have to demonstrate achievement on academic tests or fulfill any specific curriculum requirements.

Public schools are still the best place for children to get an education. They promote student achievement successfully because of the strong system of accountability behind them, which home schools do not have.

Furthermore, public schools offer many worthwhile experiences and opportunities not available through home schooling.

Teachers are highly qualified

The most important reason public schools provide an excellent education is that teachers are required to be highly qualified. They must acquire and maintain a license to teach. In order to earn this teaching certification, they must demonstrate proficiency in all basic skills, study their subject area in depth, learn effective techniques of instructing all kinds of learners and get on-the-job training under the guidance of an experienced teacher.

To maintain their license, they must continue their own education and training throughout their entire teaching career. Teachers are also held accountable by an ongoing process of evaluation. State laws that provide the requirements for teacher certification and evaluation are regularly reviewed and updated. On the other hand, there are no requirements that parents doing home schooling be trained, experienced, certified or evaluated—or have any particular qualifications.

Public schools are held accountable

The accountability in public education is also extensive in the area of academic standards. Public-school students must demonstrate adequate academic achievement.

Colorado public schools have rigorous content standards required for all academic areas, and schools' success in upholding the standards is evaluated by regular statewide and district testing. This process has been strengthened by [a July 1998] law directing the state to base its accreditation of school districts primarily on their performance in the assessment program.

No home, no matter how well equipped, can duplicate the nurturing and coping experience of a public school education.

On the other hand, home-schooled students are not required to demonstrate academic achievement on the state assessments, and their curriculum is not compelled to include any standards.

Public education in Colorado is enhanced by another kind of accountability as well, one that calls for involvement of parents and community members in school improvement planning. All schools and school districts in the state are required by law to have a committee of parents, teachers, administrators and community members. These "accountability committees" must evaluate the success of the school or district in providing for student achievement and a safe learning environment, and they advise on strategies for improvement. They are also charged with consulting on the use of taxpayers' money in the budget.

The input from the diversity of people making up these committees provides public schools with a kind of broad oversight and opportunity for new ideas not available to home schools.

Basic values are maintained

Besides the kinds of accountability already mentioned, public schools also provide a commitment to building and maintaining the basic values of our society and our democratic system of government. The Colorado Constitution provides for a "thorough and uniform system of free public schools."

The people who govern public schools are elected by the public and expected to uphold the shared values of the community. School board members receive frequent and regular feedback from the public about their management of the district.

Also, principals, teachers and other school staff receive feedback from parents, parent groups and accountability committees. The public ensures that there is ideological control over public schools.

In home schools, there is no assurance that values such as citizenship and acceptance of diversity will be encouraged. The importance of these values to our nation's survival prompted our founding fathers to support the right to a free education.

Students learn social skills

In addition to instilling values related to citizenship and acceptance of others, public schools boost children's development of social skills and employability skills that are critical to their becoming successful adults.

Because the classes in public schools are large, students are not "spoon-fed." They are forced to take more responsibility for their learning; this helps them gain more independence and initiative, which makes them better employees.

Children in public schools have to deal with many different personalities and temperaments, helping them acquire the skills to interact with the diversity of people in the world at large. They also learn to adapt to the varied leadership styles of teachers. Home-schooled children experience a homogenous group of people, sometimes only their parents.

Public schools help children become more cultured, discriminating and enlightened because they have a wide variety of resources and activities. Schools have music, sports, clubs and other student groups that give children an opportunity to learn more than pure academics and have many kinds of experiences.

Despite the few recent incidents of violence, public schools do provide children with a safe environment in which to learn. In fact, many more incidents of children's gun deaths occur in homes.

Gully Stanford, member of the Colorado Board of Education, explains best why public education surpasses home schooling. "In an increasingly diverse and technological society, the paramount need is to prepare our youth for productive citizenship: No home, no matter how well equipped, can duplicate the nurturing and coping experience of a public school education," he said.

6

Children Who Are Home Schooled Succeed Academically

Brian C. Anderson

Brian C. Anderson is senior editor of City Journal, *the cultural and political quarterly published by the Manhattan Institute.*

With its glowing academic successes, home schooling stands as a criticism of public schools. Undemanding assignments from inadequate teachers contribute to the lack of academic excellence in public schools and are the primary reasons parents home school their children. In contrast, an abundance of excellent materials can be tailored to the needs of each home-schooled child and presented in a flexible format. Outsourcing is available for difficult subjects or those subjects requiring expensive equipment. As a result of superior educational opportunities, children who are home schooled perform better on standardized exams than do students attending public schools. Parents also home school for religious reasons, finding public schools uncivil, unsafe, disorderly, and peer-dominated. Home schoolers see themselves as family-oriented and as pitted against a "me-first" American culture. Any criticism of home schoolers' lack of socialization is unfounded.

Home schooling first showed up on the national radar screen in 1997, when 13-year-old Rebecca Sealfon, all brains and awkward gestures, won the National Spelling Bee, showing a startled public that her unorthodox education must be doing something right. Today, though home schooling accounts for only 3 or 4 percent of America's schoolchildren, the movement's brisk 15 percent annual growth rate has become a powerful, hard to ignore indictment of the nation's academically underachieving, morally irresolute, disorderly, and often scary public schools. Side by side with public education's lackluster results, the richness of home schooling's achievement—the wealth of challenging subjects its pupils learn, the inculcates, the strong characters it seems to form, and the nurturing family life it reinforces—embodies a practical ideal of childhood and education that can serve as a useful benchmark of what is possible in turn-of-the-millennium America.

Though existing data are incomplete, everything we know about home-schooled kids says that they are flourishing academically in every way. [In 2000], home-schooled kids swept the top three places on the National Spelling Bee, and Stanford accepted 27 percent of its home-schooled applicants, nearly twice its average acceptance rate. Small wonder that the public school establishment wants to regulate home schooling out of existence. It represents a silent, but eloquent, reproach to the professionals.

Everything we know about home-schooled kids says that they are flourishing academically in every way.

Only 20 years ago, home schooling was a far-out fringe phenomenon. No more than 50,000 children were then educated outside of school, their parents mostly graying hippies who wanted to protect them from what they considered the stifling conformity of "the system." In the early eighties, though, the ranks of home schoolers began to swell with Christian fundamentalists dissatisfied with value-free public schools. Today, the full array of American families—from religiously orthodox Catholics and Jews to thoroughgoing secularists—are joining the fundamentalists and the Age-of-Aquarius types in home schooling their kids.

Former Department of Education researcher Patricia M. Lines, writing in *The Public Interest*, estimates that now anywhere from 1.5 to 2 million children are being home schooled, considerably more than the 400,000 students enrolled in charter schools across the country. "The rise of home schooling," Lines judges, "is one of the most significant social trends of the past half century."

A typical home schooling family

What does a typical home-schooling family look like? It is likely to be white (only 6 percent of home-schooling families are minorities) and observantly Christian, with married parents and three or more kids. The parents are likely to be better educated than the adult population at large, and the family will be comfortably middle-class—though either Mom (in nine out of ten home-schooling families) or Dad forgoes a second family income to stay at home. Mom and Dad will probably vote Republican.

The Imperatos of Bohemia, in New York's Suffolk County, fit the typical home-schooling family profile pretty much to a T. Blunt-spoken Joe Imperato, Brooklyn born and bred, works for the New York City Fire Department; his soft-spoken, articulate wife, Karen, teaches the kids, eight of them (aged 11 months to 17 years) . . . and counting. The Imperatos have been home schooling for eight years now, for academic, religious (they're evangelical Christians), and familial reasons. To get a sense of what home schooling was like up close, I went to visit them in late May.

Welcomed into their big white house with a firm handshake from Joe, I felt for a moment—no exaggeration—as if I had entered Laura Ingalls Wilder's little house on the prairie, relocated to a leafy New York suburb. The well-dressed, polite, and cheerful children spill out of every corner of the house to greet me; family portraits and drawings by the kids adorn the walls. The home radiates warmth and good order, from the kids' elaborate chore chart to the piano in the living room to the prominently displayed "House Rules" (Rule No. 1: "I Will Not Argue with Mom and Dad").

Recovering from my intrusion, the Imperatos' home school soon bustles. The family has converted one section of the house into three makeshift classrooms. There's a narrow room with a long counter for the younger kids, three of whom, 12-year-old Julie, Philip (9), and Peter (7), return to math after saying hello; a wider room humming with slightly bruised computers where Luke, 14, is doing a grammar program on CD-ROM; and a third, "quiet" room, where the older children can read. Books pile on shelves in each of the rooms, and everywhere you turn there's something to engage the mind—a wall poster time-lining major events of world history, globes, and educational videos.

The school day, Karen explains, begins promptly at 9:00, after breakfast and chores, and can last, with breaks, until 4:30. She hovers over the younger children, making sure they're working and helping them with difficult problems; Luke and 16-year-old Christine don't need much supervision. Last week, Karen informs me, the whole family dissected a frog as part of a complete science lesson purchased from an educational vendor, formaldehyde-soaked amphibian and dissecting tools included. To teach their children, the Imperatos use a mix of pre-designed curricula, including the excellent Saxon Math program, and their own improvisations. The children do well academically, says Joe; Karen beams that Philip is the equivalent of a grade ahead in math. Speaking with Luke about his American history lessons, I'm surprised at how well-informed and thoughtful he is for his age.

Though family is central for the Imperatos—the children clearly revere their folks, and Mom and Dad are proud parents—the kids do plenty outside the house, too. Christine is an accomplished pianist and Luke is getting there with the violin. They both play classical music in a home-school orchestra that meets several times a month. "*Everybody* learns to play a musical instrument in this house," laughs their father. Three of the kids, including Julie, play Little League baseball. Every month, the family spends an afternoon at the Bowery Mission helping the down-and-out. Field trips and outings with other home-schooling families are frequent. The Imperatos also participate actively in the life of the Gospel Community Church in West Sable.

I left impressed: if home schooling is responsible, even in part, for such a seemingly happy, thriving family and bright, well-mannered children, it's a big success.

The failure of public schools

The No. 1 reason that most families first decide on home schooling these days, surveys show, is dissatisfaction with the academic quality of the public schools. "A lot of parents say, I'd be happy to trust the local school system with the education of my kids—except that they haven't learned to read yet," says Susan Wise Bauer, co-author, with her mother, Jessie Wise, of *The Well-Trained Mind,* a remarkable compendium of information designed to help home-schooling parents give their children a traditional liberal education. "Something has changed in the schools for the worse over the last 20 years," believes Catherine Moran, director of a national network for Catholic home schoolers. "They're dumbing down the kids, and the teachers aren't of the highest caliber, to say the least."

Sabrina and Gary Matteson's story of their son Myles's public school woes is typical. Several years back, Myles, bored crazy with third grade at the New Hampshire public school he attended, begged his parents to let him stay home and read more challenging books—"a request from a kid that a parent shouldn't simply ignore," says Sabrina. When the Mattesons informed the school principal that they were going to home school their son, the honest administrator couldn't blame them. "He told us that they had to teach to the 40th percentile," Sabrina remembers—meaning that classroom instruction geared itself to the worst students, and sharp kids like Myles lose out. Trapped in dull public school classrooms that do nothing to engage their minds, the Myleses of the world frequently tune out or become disruptive. Even American Federation of Teachers president Sandra Feldman admits that public schools have to do more to challenge smart kids or risk losing them to home schooling.

Home schooling can take much less time than classroom schooling, since you don't have to stand in line, spend an hour at recess, or wait for the slowest student in class.

Home schoolers' misgivings about the public schools aren't just based on isolated cases. As education reformers William J. Bennett, Chester E. Finn Jr., and John T.E. Cribb Jr. underscore in their [November 2000] book, *The Educated Child,* the public schools have suffered at least since the mid-seventies from watered-down assignments and exams, politically correct textbooks, incompetent or lazy teachers who can't be fired because of union protection, and trendy educational fads like "New Math" that have pushed aside the three Rs. It's a toxic brew, the authors argue, that has left only one out of three public school fourth-graders reading "proficiently," 40 percent of public school eighth-graders unable to do basic math, and public school 12th-graders the worst in the industrialized world in science.

Why not send the kids to a competitive private school? Most home-schooling families can't afford it, even when a good private school is available nearby. *Weekly Standard* literary editor J. Bottum and his wife, Lorena, have decided to home school their daughter, Faith, in part for economic masons. "My wife and I are typical, I think, of that shabby-genteel class of people with more education than money and greater aspirations than resources," says Bottum. "At some point we realized that we would never be able to afford to hire anyone else to give our daughter the level of schooling with which we'd be satisfied."

But this may be to construe too negatively what for many home schoolers is an inspiring educational mission: to regain the vision of excellence that has vanished from so much of American education. Indeed, the brisk sales of Bauer and Wise's *The Well-Trained Mind* point to the longing of many parents to educate their kids in the great riches of the West that too many public schools value so lightly. Most of the home schoolers I encountered were learning Greek, Latin, and other serious subjects that most public schools have abandoned, and their history lessons emphasized imagination-stirring biographies of great, world-transforming men and women instead of the abstract and inhuman historical forces that so many dry-as-dust public school textbooks stress.

Home schooling allows flexibility

The rise of home schooling has sparked an explosion of marvelous curricula based on the ideal of a comprehensive liberal education. Upstate New Yorkers Melissa and David Fischer, both Cornell grads, home school their three children, 15, 14, and 12, with the help of one such curriculum. It's a "unit" study program, provided by the evangelical Christian educational firm Konos, that organizes studies, month by month, around common themes. (Secular and Catholic firms offer equally impressive curricula.) When I talked with the Fischers, they were exploring ancient Greece with Konos. After morning prayer, Melissa, who does most of the teaching, read and discussed Homer with the kids; later in the day, after math and before piano lessons, the family studied Greek history and even a bit of ancient Greek, at each child's own level. Konos is meaty stuff, using great books, the study of languages, and intelligently designed study guides for parents. Many home-schooling parents told me that they enjoy learning along with their kids, filling in gaps in their own educations.

Frequently, home-schooling parents design their own curricula. When done right, they can be imaginative and substantial. Kenneth Robinson, a lawyer by training, is one of the rare fathers who stays at home to teach (his wife writes and illustrates children's books in a wing of their pleasant Ware, Massachusetts, home). His self-designed curriculum uses "the best books I think available." Whitney, his 13-year-old daughter, begins her day with pre-algebra math, and then moves on to reading—Arthur Conan Doyle's collected Sherlock Holmes stories and C.S. Lewis's *Mere Christianity* are currently on the plate. Then it's time for logic. "I stress thinking skills and the ability to reason correctly, so we spend time looking at arguments and critiquing them for logical fallacies," Robinson says. In the afternoon, Robinson and his daughter were tackling [19th-century French activist] Frederick Bastiat's writings on socialism's flaws.

Home schooling, families say, allows you to tailor your educational approach to a child's interests, innate gifts, and learning style. This kind of flexibility can go too far: some in the small but growing "unschooling" wing of the home-schooling movement, inspired by 1960s educational radicals like John Holt and Ivan Illich, think that *any* adult direction will crush kids' creativity, so that parents should just facilitate whatever their children want to learn, whenever they want to learn it—replicating at home the trendy folly of the "child-centered classroom." But, kept within limits and balanced with fundamentals, a flexible approach can ignite a child's love of learning.

Lisa Kander is a Michigan home-schooling mother with four kids, ranging in age from ten to 18-year-old Beth, who now attends Brandeis University in Massachusetts on full scholarship. All of Kander's children read, write, and do math far above grade level. She attributes their success to home schooling's flexibility. "Home schooling allowed our four children to reach a readiness moment for reading skills on *their* timetables, not on an arbitrary curriculum chart," Kander says. With one child, that moment came earlier than average; with another, later.

Home schooling can take much less time than classroom schooling, since you don't have to stand in line, spend an hour at recess, or wait for the slowest student in class. "We can get accomplished in three hours what it takes a public school days to cover," says Sabrina Matteson. Freeing up time lets many home-schooled children devote lots of energy to interests like music. Two of Matteson's home-schooled children are gifted musicians: Myles, now 16, plays the bagpipes and his elder brother Tyler plays eight instruments, including the piano and the sitar. Almost every home-schooling family I talked with had musical children. Sixteen-year-old Piper Runnion-Bareford, home schooled in Deerfield, New Hampshire, practices the harp four hours a day, something that wouldn't be possible, she says, if she attended public school. Her effort—"pure joy," she says—has landed her the harpist's position in the New England Conservatory Youth Philharmonic.

Even a well-designed curriculum, along with great flexibility and efficiency, can't always substitute for expertise or for access to expansive facilities, such as science labs, that public and private school kids take for granted. For difficult subjects like advanced languages or upper-level science, most home-schooling families outsource, with the children enrolling in community-college courses or seeking out tutors in the fat home-schooling bulletins published these days in almost every part of the country. For example, Mary Eagleson, a retired college science professor in White Plains, New York, does a booming business as a science and math instructor for home schoolers, converting her porch into a makeshift science lab. In some states, including Washington and Iowa, home-schooled students can even enroll in public schools part-time, in order to take advantage of school facilities or sports programs. The schools receive partial state funding for the part-timers.

Academic achievements

All this sounds good, but how exactly do home-schooled children measure up academically to their counterparts in public and private school? The National Education Association—focusing, with its typical disingenuousness, on inputs rather than outcomes—has passed a testy resolution demanding that home-schooling parents go through "the appropriate state education licensure agency" and use only curricula "approved by the state department of education" before they receive state permission to home school. After all, if any dedicated parent can home school effectively, the teachers' unions' and ed schools' claim to the special, credentialized skills of "teaching professionals" collapses.

And indeed, the data show that the legions of parent-teachers are succeeding solidly. The largest study so far, authored for the Home School

Legal Defense Association by respected University of Maryland statistician Lawrence M. Rudner, examined some 20,000 home-schooled students from 50 states. These students scored higher on standardized tests than public and private school students in every subject and at every grade level. The longer their parents had home schooled them, the better they did. The results shocked the left-leaning Rudner, who initially believed that home schoolers were a bunch of "conservative nuts." He has changed his mind.

On standardized national tests of skills and achievement, Rudner found, home-schooled kids score better than 70 to 80 percent of all test-takers. Even more striking, he observes, "By eighth grade, the median performance of home-school students is almost four [grade] levels above that of students nationwide." By 12th grade, home-schooled students scored way up in the 92nd percentile in reading. Rudner cautions that his study doesn't compare home-schooled children, whose parents are generally richer and more educated than average, with equivalent public and private school kids. Moreover, the families whose kids he studied all sought testing materials from fundamentalist Bob Jones University, so they are a skewed sample.

The public schools . . . fail to shield children from the enticements of . . . "rotten popular culture" because few teachers and principals offer adult leadership or moral example.

Recent statistics from the SAT and ACT college entrance exams, though less impressive than Rudner's, are still solid. In 1999, students who identified themselves as home schooled scored an average of 1083 on the SAT, 67 points above the national average, and 22.7 on the ACT, compared with the national average of 21.

Sixty-nine percent of home schoolers go on to college, compared with 71 percent of grads from public high schools and 90 percent of private school grads. How do they get in without transcripts? Parents will put together portfolios with samples of their children's work and lists of their accomplishments. "If home-schooled students are required to take standardized tests, they take them," explains Cafi Cohen, a home-schooling mother and author of *And What About College?* "If they need a transcript, Mom or Dad sits down at the computer and writes up a transcript, with grades if necessary." More than two-thirds of American colleges now accept such transcripts, though some require home-schooled applicants to submit a GED or additional subject exams, and home schoolers now attend 900 colleges of all descriptions. Harvard accepts approximately ten every year. Oglethorpe in Atlanta actively recruits home schoolers.

Home-schooled undergrads do well, after the initial adjustment. Those who have enrolled at Boston University during the past four academic years, for example, have maintained a 3.3 grade-point average out of a perfect four. "Home schoolers bring certain skills—motivation, curiosity, the capacity to be responsible for their education—that high schools don't induce very well," a Stanford University admissions officer recently told the

Wall Street Journal. The consensus among admissions officers across the country, a 1997 study reports, is that home-schooled students are academically, emotionally, and socially prepared to excel in college.

The threat of popular culture

Though academic excellence is essential for home-schooling families, two-thirds have chosen this course primarily for religious and cultural reasons. For Joe and Karen Imperato, raising their kids right was crucial. "We want our children to grow up with sound characters and firm values," Joe stresses.

Protecting children from a popular culture overflowing with images of rebellion and sexual promiscuity is a key goal. "Home schoolers know that you don't have to condemn your kids to the kind of educational-formation-by-default in the rotten popular culture that so many parents seem to resign themselves to," remarks University of Tennessee historian Wilfred M. McClay, who has home schooled his two children, ages 11 and 14, with his wife, Julia, for four years now. Home-schooling mother Connie Marshner agrees: "You *can* resist the culture that so many horrible TV shows and movies promote today," she says. Home schooling, she's convinced, helps you take up arms against it: "It allows parents to play more fully the role of cultural gatekeepers," she maintains. Accordingly, only 1.6 percent of fourth-grade home schoolers watch more than three hours of television per day, compared with 40 percent of fourth-graders nationally.

The public schools, those home schoolers believe, fail to shield children from the enticements of McClay's "rotten popular culture" because few teachers and principals offer adult leadership or moral example anymore. "Teachers don't know how to discipline kids today, since they themselves don't believe in authority," Marshner argues. "The sixties destroyed the idea. How can you inculcate character and good behavior— the old idea of deportment—without legitimate authority?" Some teachers even stoke the spirit of rebellion in their young students. Laurie Runnion-Bareford began her journey toward home schooling her kids after a New Hampshire public school teacher told her ten-year-old son that profanities were okay to use in a vocabulary assignment. "It wasn't as if he hadn't heard bad words before," Runnion-Bareford recalls, "but the signal his teacher sent by doing this was that incivility was acceptable— which was unacceptable to us." Many home schoolers, too, find the *Heather Has Two Mommies* and condoms-on-bananas aspect of today's public school regime deeply offensive.

This abdication of authority, social thinkers say, has produced disorderly and uncivil schools, where the peer group sets the terms. "There used to be a social consensus that you don't talk back to adults, you don't spit, you don't swear at the teacher," Marshner says. "All those things start breaking down now in the fourth grade, as kids start taking their cues from their peers and popular culture." Says Catherine Moran of such peer-dominated schools: "Everyone acts the same, dresses the same, and, when they're 12 or 13, pierces the same—and in some cases starts having sex or doing drugs." Says social scientist Rudner: "When a nine-year-old comes home with garbage language and garbage values, home schooling makes sense."

Sabrina Matteson sees the Columbine massacre as a watershed for home schooling. "Columbine caused a lot of families and students to assess the safety of their schools," she says. Colorado's home-schooling population rose 10 percent in the months after the killings. Friends of the Mattesons just pulled all their kids out of their local New Hampshire public school after the seventh bomb scare this year.

The socialization question

Critics of home schooling claim that withdrawing children from the classroom will retard their "socialization," to use educrat jargon. Charges Annette Cootes of the NEA-affilliated Texas State Teachers Association: "[H]ome schooling is a form of child abuse because you are isolating children from human interaction. I think home schoolers are doing a great discredit [*sic*] to their children."

Yet social science research suggests that home-schooled children aren't lacking in social skills. Grad student Larry Shyers of the University of Florida videotaped at play 70 home-schooled eight- to ten-year-old children and 70 children of the same age group who attended school. Trained counselors—who watched the tapes without knowing which group the kids belonged to—found only one behavioral difference: the home-schooled kids had fewer behavior problems.

Even a cursory familiarity with home schoolers makes clear that the accusation of isolation is absurd. Most home-schooled kids take advantage of buzzing networks of associations. Beth Kander's busy social calendar as a home schooler before she left for Brandeis is typical. "I never had a problem with friends," she recounts, "since I belonged to the Girl Scouts, participated in several 4-H clubs and youth programs and the drama club my mother started, and volunteered all over the place." Many home-schooled kids join church groups, play in town sports leagues, do internships, or work part-time. And they form their own associations, everything from poetry recitation clubs to Scandinavian dance groups to home-school orchestras—legions of them.

For their part, home-schooling families reject the model of age-based socialization that the schools offer. "I don't know any adults who would choose to spend eight hours a day, five days a week with 20 to 30 people of exactly the same age," says Glorianna Pappas, a New York musician and home-schooling mother. Instead, home schoolers often meet people of widely different ages and outlooks when helping out at a homeless shelter or singing in a church choir. "This gives them a greater level of poise, experience, and maturity than can be had in the artificial confines of rigid, age-based classrooms," argues educational theorist Andrew J. Coulson.

The family bond

Still, for home schoolers, family comes first. Historian Dana Mack sees home schooling as an important example of what she believes to be a growing "familist counterculture." This counterculture firmly rejects elite culture's contempt for traditional family values and its celebration of a me-first ethic in pleasure and work that has led to sky-high divorce and illegitimacy rates and a generation of sad and neglected kids. "Home schooling," Mack holds, "is one aspect of a new vision of family life that equates family time with children's well-being, and that puts family intimacy and child-parent bonds before self-realization and economic gain."

For many, home schooling gives family life an unexpected richness. Historian McClay, who watched his teenage son Mark develop a deep love for classical music and leap ahead academically when removed from school, describes the "transformative" impact that home schooling had on his family. "There's this sense that we're involved in a project in life together: the notion that the family is an arrow in time is much more meaningful to me and to all of us than it was before," he says. "We've seen a bonding in our family that we wouldn't have seen if we didn't home school," stresses Joe Imperato. "When you become the teacher, you're really aware of the incredible responsibility you have toward your children."

Home-schooling families reject the model of age-based socialization that the schools offer.

Home schooling seems to minimize the proverbial friction between teens and their parents. "Life with our home-schooled teens has been a joy—heaven," Laurie Runnion-Bareford enthuses. "It surprised us, because my friends who had teenage kids in the public schools were miserable." But, after all, argues home schooler Douglas Dewey, Chief Operating Officer of Theodore Forstmann's Children's Scholarship Fund, "Not so long ago, it wasn't considered natural or even tolerable for children to rebel against their parents."

It's important not to over-idealize home schooling's impact on family life. It is an enormous investment of time for a teaching parent, and it can lead to burnout. Says Shari Henry, a contributing editor of *Homeschooling Today* and a home-schooling mother of three: "One February, when the weather was bad, I just said to myself, I can't keep doing this—it's too much responsibility." To avoid burnout, Henry emphasizes, home-schooling parents, particularly those with young children, must give themselves occasional breaks and make certain that they're plugged in to a good support network of other home-schooling families. In addition to this difficulty, home-schooling parents often encounter painful opposition from their own parents or from neighbors and friends. And—one last danger—Susan Wise Bauer, who speaks to home-schooling families across the country, reports that one does occasionally come across a paranoid and domineering parent, afraid of letting go—ever—of the children.

Legal challenges

The rise of home schooling has pressured the legal system to accommodate it. "From the early eighties through the next decade, there was a pitched war over whether home schooling was going to be legal at all," recalls Michael Farris, the lawyer and former politician who heads the Home Schooling Legal Defense Association. When his advocacy organization was formed in 1983, home schooling was illegal or strongly discouraged in all but three states, and school administrators and teachers' unions wanted to keep it that way. Parents who tried to teach their kids at home frequently faced jail terms and the loss of their children to foster care as school districts cracked down on them for breaking state compulsory education laws.

But because of the HSLDA, which has won virtually every legal battle it has fought, and because of the warm support of Republican legislators, home schooling is now legal in all 50 states, though the degree of state regulation varies. Texas's regulations, for example, are all but nonexistent: home-schooling parents must cover reading, spelling, grammar, math, and good citizenship, but they don't have to keep records or have their kids academically tested annually or follow any rigid timetable. New York's regulations, by contrast, require parents to teach "AIDS awareness," "substance abuse," physical education, and health (i.e., sex ed), among a host of other specific subject requirements, and they must do so on a state-determined schedule; parents must also file detailed quarterly reports with the local school superintendent. (Many states once required home-schooling parents to have teacher certification, but all have abolished that requirement.)

Nevertheless, even today, Farris complains, some school districts "just don't get it." This March, to take one egregious example of many, the Richmond County School District sent cops to arrest Gerald and Angela Balderson, after they removed their eight-year-old from his Warsaw, Virginia, public school to teach him at home. The Baldersons had scrupulously given notice to the school superintendent, as Virginia law requires. But the district chose to call out the truant officer on them nonetheless. The Baldersons, understandably, are suing. According to the HSLDA, home schoolers also have to watch out for social workers, some of whom perversely view home schooling as a "risk factor" in assessing the likelihood of a family to commit child abuse.

Against opposition like this, home schoolers have turned themselves into a formidable political force. California Democratic Congressman George Miller learned this the hard way. In 1994, he offered an amendment to a federal education bill that specified that teachers had to have certification in the subjects they taught. Miller protested that he didn't intend the amendment to apply to home schoolers, but worried home-schooling parents, galvanized into action by the HSLDA, barraged Congress with hundreds of thousands of phone calls. The amendment, which had already made it through committee, got only one vote on the floor—Miller's.

What level of regulation is appropriate for home schooling? The best arguments are on the side of a relatively laissez-faire [hands-off] approach. The New York–NEA model of constant school-district supervision and narrowly specified subject requirements implicitly presumes that the state does a good job educating kids and that parents are ignorant until proven otherwise—dubious propositions. Moreover, some states' subject requirements may offend a home-schooling family's deeply felt cultural and religious beliefs, subverting the very reason they've decided to home school their children in the first place. But the public does have a legitimate interest in making sure that home-schooled kids get educated and that, say, a dysfunctional foster care family isn't yanking its children out of school to use them as laborers. The most sensible regulations would be minimal, requiring home-schooled kids only to demonstrate—through taking a state test or some agreed-upon alternative means—that they were learning how to read, write, and do math by a certain age.

"In America in the twenty-first century," William Bennett recently observed, "no family should feel it has to educate at home to educate well." But until that day comes, home schooling will continue to grow—educating kids successfully, invigorating civil society, and reaffirming family values.

7

There Is Little Evidence That Home Schooling Is Successful

Katherine Pfleger

Katherine Pfleger is a writer for the Associated Press news service.

The growth in home schooling also increases the possibility that well-intentioned parents will deprive their children of social and academic skills. While academic accomplishments have been documented for home-schooled children, there's little evidence to suggest that home schooling is universally successful. Studies purporting to find that home-schooled children succeed academically are flawed because only some home-schooling parents participate in them. There's also anecdotal evidence that some parents are unable to cope with schooling their children at home.

Carole Kennedy is a principal at one of the local schools in Columbia, Missouri. But one of the students she says worries her the most isn't even enrolled there. "This boy was in our school in the fourth and fifth grade and had behavior problems. His parents never had an interest in his education. They'd miss parent-teacher conferences. They'd drop him off at concerts and then not pick him up. When he got to middle school, he had attendance problems. His parents got tired of the calls from the attendance office and announced that they were going to pull him out of school and teach him at home." Homeschooling laws vary widely from state to state—some require that parents follow an approved curriculum or bring in their children for annual testing. But, in Missouri, all the boy's parents have to do is file some paperwork. "Now," says Kennedy, "his former friends say he's doing nothing all day."

Stories like this may not be as rare as we'd like to imagine. Once a relatively limited phenomenon, homeschooling is on the rise. Between 1990 and 1995 the number of children taught at home more than doubled—today it stands at over one million. And, as the popularity of homeschooling continues to increase, so does the likelihood that well-meaning parents who lack the know-how, time, or resources to be effective teach-ers—or, worse, parents who actually have malign motives for keeping their kids out of school—will deprive their children of needed social skills and a decent education.

Greater acceptance

Homeschooling used to be the province of the religious right. During the 1980s, Christian conservatives seized on it as a way to insulate their chil-dren from what they perceived to be the anti-family culture of public schools. These parents, generally full-time mothers, relied on religious groups to provide them with a curriculum and contacts with other home-schooling families. But, over the past few years, homeschooling has spread well beyond the Christian right; a multitude of Muslim, Jewish, African American, secular, and other homeschooling organizations are popping up across the country. And homeschooling has become an in-creasingly respected option. Between 1985 and 1997, the percentage of Americans who said they approved of it increased from 16 to 36 percent. Homeschooling, in short, has gone mainstream.

The public needs to hear about the overextended mothers.

What accounts for the trend? In some cases parents see homeschool-ing as a remedy for the overcrowded classrooms, cookie-cutter curricula, and indifferent teachers that plague so many public school systems. In other cases parents don't trust the public schools to educate their little ge-niuses, or perhaps they have a child who has been diagnosed with a learn-ing disability and want to customize his education to meet his needs. Pri-vate schooling used to be the solution to many of these problems. But, at just a couple of hundred dollars a year for texts and learning materials, homeschooling is a better bargain.

And, to be sure, homeschooling is not necessarily a prescription for domestic disaster. In fact, there are some stunning success stories. Take Andy of Washington, D.C., who is marching through the fourth-grade curriculum of the Calvert School in Baltimore—one of several reputable correspondence schools that offers graders, transcripts, and diplomas to homeschoolers. Andy is a sweet and highly social kid. He participates in a chess club, arts-and-crafts classes, and group field trips. He has studied the stock market and Latin. He is fascinated by idioms. All this, at seven years old.

Flawed research

But, while homeschooling enthusiasts insist that children taught at home score higher on tests and get into better colleges, a closer look at the re-search suggests there is little evidence either way. What few studies have been done may be flawed. The most commonly cited study, sponsored by the National Home Education Research Institute, is a case in point. According to that report, the average public school student scores in the 50th percentile on national tests, while the average homeschooler scores in the 80th to 87th percentile—regardless of race. That sounds like an open-and-shut case for homeschooling. But Glen Cutlip, an official of the National Education Association, points out that the study averages percentiles from several different tests, comparing the scores of homeschoolers nationwide with those of public school students from only the state of Virginia. In addition, he says, since the homeschoolers were selected by sending out a questionnaire, they constitute a self-selected group, not a representative sample of the entire homeschooling population.

And there's the rub. In order to assess homeschooling's effectiveness, researchers need full access to homeschooled children. Unfortunately, many homeschooling parents—particularly those in the religious right, who are also the most organized group within the movement—are vehemently opposed to any outside interference. They even have a lobby, part of the 50,000-member Home School Legal Defense Association, dedicated to blocking the logical next step that would follow further studies: the creation of national standards that would ensure all homeschooled kids are getting at least a rudimentary education.

Not that the homeschoolers need to worry about a serious challenge to their autonomy. The Department of Education has traditionally left the administration of compulsory education to local government, and it shows no inclination to get involved now. As for the press, it has been too busy touting homeschooling miracles to look at the movement critically. But, instead of glowing descriptions of seven-year-old prodigies, the public needs to hear about the overextended mothers, like the one I interviewed, while she juggled a telephone, a toddler screaming for a piece of string cheese, and a second-grader she was supposed to be homeschooling. And the public needs to hear about the public school teachers, like several in the Missouri school, who, Carole Kennedy says, are struggling to reeducate a student who fell several grades behind during the two years his mother taught him at home. This child's remedial education will cost the taxpayers money. That, if nothing else, should get the public's attention.

8

Home-Schooled Students Are Well Socialized

William R. Mattox Jr.

William R. Mattox Jr. is a journalist and member of the board of contributors for USA Today. He writes regularly on family issues for major newspapers and magazines in the United States.

On average each week, home-schooled children are involved with at least five social activities outside the home. With participation in these activities, they interact with more people of differing ages, which is more like the "real world." Additionally, home-schooled children identify socially with their family more so than with their peers, resulting in less alienation and isolation and producing higher self-esteem. In particular, home-schooled adolescent girls are less likely to lose self-confidence when their friends don't agree with their opinions.

Most folks who have never met a homeschooling family imagine that the kids are about as socially isolated (and as socially awkward) as Bobby Boucher, the Cajun "Momma's boy" Adam Sandler portrays in the recent hit film, *The Waterboy.*

But some new research by Brian Ray of the National Home Education Research Institute suggests otherwise. Indeed, Ray's research helps to explain why the number of homeschoolers in America continues to grow and now totals more than 1.4 million children.

The homeschooler's social life

Ray reports the typical homeschooled child is involved in 5.2 social activities outside the home each week. These activities include afternoon and weekend programs with conventionally schooled kids, such as ballet classes, Little League teams, Scout troops, church groups and neighborhood play. They include midday field trips and cooperative learning programs organized by groups of homeschooling families. For example, some Washington, D.C., families run a homeschool drama troupe that performs at a local dinner theater.

So, what most distinguishes a homeschooler's social life from that of a conventionally schooled child? Ray says homeschooled children tend to interact more with people of different ages.

This is actually more akin to the "real world"—what businessperson's social interaction is largely restricted to those born in the same year? It reduces the degree to which children find themselves constantly being compared to, and comparing themselves with, other kids their age. Interestingly, this reduced consciousness about age tends to help homeschooled "late bloomers" avoid being stigmatized as "slow learners"— which is one of the many reasons homeschoolers, on average, score 30 to 37 percentile points higher than conventionally schooled students on the most commonly administered K–8 standardized tests.

The homeschooler's social identity

Moreover, homeschooled children tend to draw their primary social identity from their membership in a particular family rather than from their membership in "a tribe apart." That's the phrase author Patricia Hersch uses to describe the conventionally schooled kids she followed through adolescence.

According to Hersch, many school kids today feel isolated from the grown-up world and alienated from parents who fail to take an interest in their lives and to set boundaries for their behavior.

Now, Hersch's intention isn't to make a case for homeschooling. (She doesn't significantly address the issue.) But the angst-ridden teens she describes in her book closely resemble the peer-obsessed students Seattle public high school teacher David Guterson talks about in his compelling book, *Family Matters: Why Homeschooling Makes Sense.*

Many school kids today feel isolated from the grownup world and alienated from parents who fail to take an interest in their lives.

Guterson reports that the kids in his conventional school often have difficulty navigating the turbulent social scene at school, with "its cliques, rumors and relentless gossip, its shifting alliances and expedient betrayals." Guterson says that their preoccupation with peer acceptance often encourages young people to become "accurately attuned to a pre-adult commercial culture that usurps their attention (M-TV, Nintendo, fashion magazines, teen cinema)" and frequently fosters a sense of alienation from people of other ages.

Interestingly, educational researcher Susannah Sheffer of Cambridge, Mass., says facilitating peer-dependency is part of "how schools short-change girls" (to borrow the title of a highly publicized report issued [in 1992] by the American Association of University Women). In a recent study of self-esteem among adolescent gifts, Sheffer found that unlike their conventionally schooled counterparts, homeschooled girls did not typically lose confidence in themselves when their ideas and opinions weren't embraced by their friends.

Now, none of this means that every homeschooler is socially well-adjusted. Or that homeschooling is the only way for parents to raise children successfully. Or that good things never happen in conventional schools. But these studies do suggest that homeschooling offers more than just educational benefits. No wonder a growing number of families are now giving home education a try.

9

Home Schooling Deprives Children of Important Social Lessons

Gillian Bowditch

Gillian Bowditch is a correspondent for the Sunday Times *(London).*

Home education is not a reasonable choice for most children, as they need to spend time with peer groups to fulfill social needs. While home-schooled students may succeed academically, they may also fail to achieve that sense of independence generally acquired when attending public school. Additionally, home-schooled children may not learn problem-solving skills that are normally acquired through everyday interaction in public school circumstances.

Back to the chalkface [blackboard] this week—but for thousands of Scotland's school-aged children there will be none of the familiar little rituals that mark the start of a new term. There will be no last-minute scrabbling to finish the holiday homework, no family search party to track down a recalcitrant gym shoe and no howling at 8.30 A.M. over the lack of a clean shirt.

Nor will there be a qualified teacher to educate them, access to a science laboratory, PE department, school orchestra, choir, nativity play, carol concert, end-of-term disco, team games, sports day, inter-school competitions or school outing.

They do not have to follow the national curriculum, have formal lessons, observe school hours or keep to a fixed timetable. Most will never see a school inspector. These are the children who are being educated at home.

An educational utopia?

Read anything on educating children at home and you will stumble upon a new world, a kind of educational utopia.

Home-educated children are invariably described as bright and inquisitive. They love learning and are never bored. While "normal" school youngsters flop on the sofa with a Game Boy and yell for industrial quantities of sweets, home-educated children are knocking up an electrical circuitry kit and tucking into the baking which was the result of that afternoon's lesson about weights and measures.

Sifting through many accounts I found only one mother who admitted to problems. Angela Pollard, a teacher, educated her 13-year-old twins at home for six months before they begged to go back to school. At first it worked well. Their knowledge grew in [Olympic triple-jumper] Jonathan Edwards–sized leaps—but the twins grew increasingly lonely.

We should no more encourage the home educators than we should advocate that parents prescribe their children's medication or fill their teeth.

Discipline was difficult. The roles of mother and teacher became blurred. The children resented being made to study maths by mum. It took them a year to settle back into school but even at their lowest ebb they were adamant that they wanted to stay in the system.

Pollard's is a lone voice. Home educators are a highly motivated, evangelical group fighting for their rights to bring up their children in the way they feel is best. Their propaganda is well honed. The subliminal message is: educate at home and you get Little House on the Prairie; send your children to the local school and you get The Royal Family.

They are winning more converts than a [evangelist] Billy Graham rally. Home education started off as a slightly wacky, alternative lifestyle for a handful of hippie families in the 1970s. Now it is estimated there are 5,000 children being taught at home in Scotland. Only 350 of them are registered with local authorities.

The vast majority, it seems, have never been sent to school in the first place which, while perfectly legal, means that the authorities have no idea who they are or what sort of education they are receiving.

Now the Scottish executive is attempting to trace them using birth registers, census information and health visitor records. Guidelines are being drafted. In the future, home-educated children should have their learning more closely monitored.

You would think that the home educators would welcome these steps. If, as they claim, they have a system that is superior to state education, there is nothing to fear. Instead they are claiming that interference from the authorities is breaching their human rights. Alison Preuss, spokeswoman for the home education charity Schoolhouse, called the government's plans "a bully's charter." However, education authorities have a duty to ensure that children are being properly taught, and if Preuss's level of paranoia is typical, alarm bells should be ringing. The executive is right to be concerned.

Home education may be a sensible choice for a minority of children who are deeply unhappy at school or whose needs are so extreme that they cannot be met by mainstream education, but it cannot be the sensible option for most children.

You have to wonder who is really the main beneficiary of home education. The child, or the parents who demand total control of their offspring's life?

As Pollard says: "I didn't take into account one basic need—that children need to be with their peers. That is as vital to their personal growth as the subjects they learn. I could meet all their educational needs but I couldn't come close to satisfying their social needs. If I'd continued with it, I would have been doing it for myself, not for them."

Of course, home-educated children will learn and may outstrip their peers in tests. The undivided attention of an enthusiastic parent who is prepared to let you chop your way through the contents of the fruit bowl in an effort to understand fractions is bound to produce results. But school is not just about learning facts and figures. It is about interacting with your peers in all sorts of situations. It is about separating from your parents and developing your own tastes, beliefs and interests. Just ask Ruth Lawrence, the home-educated child genius who went to Oxford at 12 and ended up alienated from her stifling, overbearing father.

A taste of independence

Home educators who claim that their children have plenty of friends and social contacts miss the point. School is a child's first taste of independence, the first chance to discover they are not the centre of the universe and to adapt accordingy. These fundamental friendships and experiences cannot be replicated in the home with the help of a textbook on creative education and a borrowed Bunsen burner.

Our schools may not be perfect but that is partly the point. No child will sail through their education without encountering some problem, whether it be bullying, bad teaching or difficulty in learning. How a child, with the help of supportive parents and school, responds to these problems and overcomes them is as valuable a part of the educational process as learning to read and write.

The trend towards home education is another symptom of the "little emperor" syndrome. We are in danger of producing a generation of cloistered, mollycoddled children for whom the best is not quite good enough. These are children who do not know how to assess risk or overcome problems because their parents simply magic away all hazards or unpleasantness.

Our education system, whatever its faults, has been honed over centuries. Our teachers are highly qualified professionals. If schools were not the vital and valuable heart of our community, why would rural populations fight so hard to save them? Parents unhappy with the system should work to change it or move to a country where there is no state education and see how progressive that feels.

We should no more encourage the home educators than we should advocate that parents prescribe their children's medication or fill their teeth.

10

Home Schooling Affects Families Positively

Kate Tsubata

Kate Tsubata is a freelance writer who home schools her three children.

Home schooling has a positive effect on the family dynamic, creating greater togetherness than is usually found in traditionally schooled families. This togetherness occurs because parents are perceived by their children as sources of knowledge rather than as judges. Without the pressure to earn grades, both parents and children can concentrate on learning, and every situation can, therefore, become an opportunity to learn. Overall, home-schooling families are innovative, spontaneous, and mother-centered, and home-schooled children are self-confident.

D o you remember this phrase from a hair-color commercial, "Is it true blondes have more fun?" Well, I sometimes get the guilty feeling that home scholars just have more fun.

I have come to this conclusion after participating in a few events with other home-schooling families. At an event in which most folks would be sitting down, cool and quiet, the home scholars are almost always active, participating with all their might.

A typical home-schooling event

At a recent concert hosted by home-schooling families in Montgomery County, folks of all ages were singing, dancing and even jumping on a trampoline. Parents and children both were having a ball. No one was "shushing" anyone, and the band did not want to stop playing. How many audiences of parents and children have you seen having such a great time together?

At a Fourth of July barbecue, several home-schooling families shared the usual hot dogs and hamburgers, and the children played basketball and other games. But when we brought out a Jell-O mold in the shape of the United States, we all spontaneously began singing "The Star-Spangled

Banner." The children loved it. When we went to cut the Jell-O to serve it, the youngsters each asked for the state of their choice: "I want Texas! I want Florida! I want California!"

One of the mothers then led a discussion about George Washington and some of the other heroes of the Revolutionary War. The children volunteered anecdotes and stories they had studied. Although the discussion was initially meant for the "10 and older" crowd, most of the younger brothers and sisters, and all the parents, were so curious that they all sat in on the storytelling.

After an hour of swapping tales, everyone piled into cars and trekked over to a local fireworks spectacle. No one wanted to leave, despite the late hour.

Home-schooling means working, learning and playing as a family.

This is a far cry from the many families I see around me, in which parents' suggestions are greeted with groans from the children, and the children lobby their parents for a long list of demands that are "peer only" activities. The negotiations go on forever, and whatever the outcome, someone is unhappy.

The idea that parents would lead a discussion on the heroes of the Revolutionary War—and that their children would participate enthusiastically—would seem like an exercise in fantasy to many.

Positive effects

Many home-schooling families have told me about the positive effects of home education on the family dynamic. Parents and children just get along better. The situation is very different from the nagging that most parents have to do to get their children to complete homework assignments or to study for tests. In home education, parents and children are working toward a common goal. Children see parents as resources and teachers, not as ride providers and grade judges.

Conversely, parents are able to view the child's learning process firsthand. They see the child's study habits, discoveries and daily work. Without the worry of "getting an A," both the child and the parent can focus on the main job of learning. And, strange as it seems, learning is a lot of fun. In fact, it is impossible to stop the habit of learning once it has begun.

When families develop the learning habit, everything becomes interesting and a chance for discovery. Lately, our family has become fascinated with the moon. As we are driving somewhere at night, we start asking questions: Why do we only see one face of the moon? How long does it take for the moon to rotate on its axis? What would happen if the moon did not exist? Does the moon help stabilize the Earth?

Our questions turn into quests. The quests turn into research. And the research produces answers, which are very satisfying when they are the result of one's own search.

Quite by chance, my son received an interesting book with a section on the moon for his birthday. He discovered the answers to the family's musings and was very excited to tell the rest of us.

The home-schooling family

I think that home-schooling families have more fun because they are working together and playing together. So many learning opportunities occur every day which involve members of the family that you cannot help but develop more closeness, more involvement with one another. So parents stay young, and children are comfortable with adults. Also, older and younger siblings cooperate, which makes things more harmonious.

For these reasons, we cannot relate to the relationships portrayed on most comedy programs, in which children sabotage and demean one another and the parents vacillate between being wimpy and being authoritarian. It just seems odd, like observing a foreign culture.

I do believe a home-schooling culture is developing, with its own patterns, values and dynamics. At the risk of generalizing, I would say that most home-schooling families are curious about new things, willing to buck trends, highly communicative and spontaneous. They tend to be mother-centered (in the actual schooling), but fathers also tend to be more involved with their children's learning than in the average, traditionally schooled family.

Home-schooling families are innovative, often creating independent study opportunities out of community or private events. Students seem to be more aware that the information they are gaining has value in their daily lives.

There seems to be virtually no categorizing of others into subsets such as "nerd," "jock," "popular" or "stupid." For this reason, home scholars have plenty of self-confidence and do not feel compelled to efface themselves for protection nor to affect certain behaviors to be accepted.

All of which makes it easier to deal with life in an enjoyable way. Home-schooling means working, learning and playing as a family. The family is not something you spend your time with only outside school or work. Rather, it is where you are, all the time.

11

Home Schooling May Hide Parental Instability or Abuse

Froma Harrop

Froma Harrop is a syndicated columnist.

Because home-schooled children are isolated from the community, home schooling hides any evidence of instability and child abuse within the family. A number of high-profile cases of home-schooling parents abusing their children highlights the need for more extensive evaluation of home schooling's effects on children. Home-schooling advocates garner support for alternative education by arguing that home-schooled children score high academically. However, these students generally come from upper-income, well-educated families, the types of families whose children also perform well in public schools.

America's most famous home-schooling parents at the moment are Andrea Yates and JoAnn McGuckin. Yates allegedly drowned her five children in a Houston suburb. McGuckin was arrested and charged with child neglect in Idaho. Her six kids barricaded themselves in the family's hovel when child-care workers came to remove them.

The intention here is not to smear the parents who instruct 1.5 million mostly normal children at home. But a social phenomenon that isolates children from the outside world deserves closer inspection.

Home-schooling propaganda

The home-schooling movement runs an active propaganda machine. It portrays its followers in the most flattering terms—as bulwarks against the moral decay found in public, and presumably private, schools. Although now associated with conservative groups, modern home-schooling got its start among left-wing dropouts in the '60s.

Home-schooled students do tend to score above average on standardized tests. The most likely reason, however, is that most of the parents are themselves upper income and well educated. Students from those backgrounds also do well in traditional schools.

Advocates of home-schooling have become a vocal lobbying force in Washington, D.C. Children taught at home may be socially isolated, but the parents have loads of interaction. Membership in the anti-public-education brigade provides much comradeship.

The mouthpiece for the movement, the Home School Legal Defense Association (www.hslda.org), posts articles on its Web site with headlines like, "The Clinging Tentacles of Public Education." Trashing the motivations of professional teachers provides much sport.

A movement that insists on parents' rights to do as they wish with their children gives cover for the unstable, for narcissists and for child-abusers.

Perhaps the time has come to question the motives of some home-schooling parents. Are the parents protecting their children from a cesspool of bad values in the outside world? Or are the parents just people who can't get along with others? Are they "taking charge" of their children's education? Or are they taking their children captive?

Yates and McGuckin are, of course, extreme cases and probably demented. But a movement that insists on parents' rights to do as they wish with their children gives cover for the unstable, for narcissists and for child-abusers.

A case of child endangerment

In West Akron, Ohio, reporters would interview Thomas Lavery on how he successfully schooled his five children in their home. The kids all had top grades and fine manners. They recalled how their father loved to strut before the media.

Eventually, however, the police came for Lavery and charged him with nine counts of child endangerment. According to his children, Lavery smashed a daughter over the head with a soda can after she did poorly in a basketball game. Any child who wet a bed would spend the night alone, locked in the garage.

A child who spilled milk had to drop on his or her knees and lick it up from the floor. And in an especially creepy attempt to establish himself as master, Lavery would order his children to damn the name of God.

The best way to maintain the sanctity of a family madhouse is to keep the inmates inside. Allowing children to move about in the world could jeopardize the deal.

Preventing tragedy

In some cases, it might also prevent tragedy. Suppose one of Andrea Yates' children had gone to a school and told a teacher of the mother's spiraling mental state. The teacher could have called a child-welfare officer and five little lives might have been saved.

Putting the horror stories aside, there's something sad about home-schooled children. During the New Hampshire presidential primary race, I attended an event directed at high-school and college students. The students were a lively bunch, circulating around the giant room, debating and arguing. Except for my table.

About four young people and a middle-aged woman were just sitting there. The teenagers were clearly intelligent and well behaved. I tried to chat, but they seemed wary of talking with strangers. The woman proudly informed me that they were her children and home-schooled.

The Home School Legal Defense Association condemns government interference in any parent's vision of how a child might be educated. The group's chairman, Michael Farris, says things like, "We just want to say to the government: We are doing a good job, so leave us alone."

Could that be where JoAnn McGuckin found her twisted sense of grievance? "Those are my kids," she said as Idaho removed her children from their filthy home. "The state needs to mind its own business."

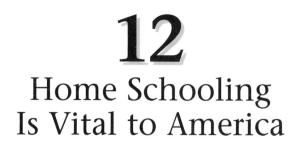

Home Schooling
Is Vital to America

Samuel L. Blumenfeld

Samuel L. Blumenfeld is a columnist for the WorldNetDaily *and is the author of eight books, including* Is Public Education Necessary? *and* NEA: Trojan Horse in American Education.

Liberal humanists seek, through the state, to take control of children by denying parents the right to educate them. In subordinating the family unit to government and by interfering in affairs usually resolved between church and family, humanists are playing God. Home schooling restores this country to the way the Founding Fathers envisioned it because home-schooled children are free from humanist teachings. Through home education, families are made stronger. Children are instilled with a higher moral standard and protected from the negative influences of drugs and sex prevalent in public schools. Home-schooling families must remain politically active to protect their right to home school.

We Americans are a very special breed. Something in our psyche, in our culture has set us apart from other nations. In fact, people in other countries cannot understand why so many Americans have such a deep distrust of government. But when these foreigners arrive in this country as immigrants and expect to find themselves in the land of the free and the home of the brave, they find themselves in the land of bureaucratic regulation and educational confusion.

They settle in cities where the crime rate is much higher than in the countries they left. Yet, few return to their countries of origin because they detect something in America that is different and not to be found anywhere else: the deep sense of hope, an indefatigable entrepreneurial spirit, boundless energy, the religious fervor of millions of individuals who are trying indeed to restore America to what it once was: a nation under God, a land of unlimited opportunity and limited, unobtrusive government bound by a Constitution based on Biblical principles. Ayn Rand, the novelist, put it in these words:

From Samuel L. Blumenfeld's speech delivered at the Montana Homeschool Association Conference in Great Falls, August 11, 1995. Copyright © 1995 by Samuel L. Blumenfeld. Reprinted with permission.

"The most profoundly revolutionary achievement of the United States of America was the subordination of society to moral law."

That moral law, of course, was Biblical law. Early visitors to America remarked on that aspect of the American way of life. Alexis de Tocqueville, the French historian who visited America in the 1830s, wrote:

"Upon my arrival in the United States the religious aspect of the country was the first thing that struck my attention; and the longer I stayed there, the more I perceived the great political consequences resulting from this state of things. . . .

"In the United States the sovereign authority is religious . . . there is no country in the world where the Christian religion retains a greater influence over the souls of men than in America, and there can be no greater proof of its utility and of its conformity to human nature than that its influence is powerfully felt over the most enlightened and free nation of the earth.

"Christianity, therefore reigns without obstacle, by universal consent; the consequence is, as I have before observed, that every principle of the moral world is fixed and determinate . . . .

"The safeguard of morality is religion, and morality is the best security of law as well as the surest pledge of freedom.

"Not until I went into the churches of America and heard her pulpits flame with righteousness did I understand the secret of her genius and power.

"America is great because America is good, and if America ever ceases to be good, America will cease to be great."

The humanist philosophy

How far we have come from that benevolent state in which Biblical law set the moral standards of American society. Today, what we have in America is the subordination of society to bureaucratic law, the law of the state. Yes, these laws were enacted by the legislators we elect. But too many of these legislators no longer believe in the primacy of Biblical law. They believe that man's law is superior to God's law. We call that philosophy humanism, and that's the philosophical foundation of liberalism.

Liberalism goes under many guises: progressivism, socialism, collectivism. No matter what you call it, its most significant principle is its rejection of God as the true sovereign over our nation. And, of course, this has serious consequences for the family and for education.

Humanism is an organized religious-philosophical movement dedicated to the overthrow of Christianity. The humanists declared war on Christianity in 1933 with the proclamation of its Humanist Manifesto which states:

"Religious humanism maintains that all associations and institutions exist for the fulfillment of human life. The intelligent evaluation, transformation, control, and direction of
such associations and institutions with a view to the en-
hancement of human life is the purpose and program of humanism. Certainly religious institutions, their ritualistic
forms, ecclesiastical methods, and communal activities must
be reconstituted as rapidly as experience allows, in order to
function effectively in the modern world."

In other words, the humanist program calls for taking control of and
transforming all of the cultural and religious institutions and associations
of the nation so that they will be made to effectively advance the humanist agenda. No other religion in America calls for taking over the institutions and associations of other religions. We are supposed to be living in a society where religious freedom is respected by all religions. But
we have it in the words of the Humanist Manifesto itself the intention of
humanists to reconstitute everybody else's religious institutions, rituals,
and ecclesiastical practices to conform with humanist goals.

The threat of humanism

Nowhere has the philosophical conflict between humanism and Christianity been better explained than in Dr. Rousas J. Rushdoony's classic
book, the *Messianic Character of American Education,* for it is in the field of
education that the conflict has raced most intensely. It should be noted
that one of the signers of the Humanist Manifesto of 1933 was John
Dewey, father of progressive education.

*One of the most important actions families can take
is to remove their children from the government
schools and homeschool them.*

Dr. Rushdoony shows that humanism not only threatens Christian
education but educational freedom in general, because there is a link between religious liberty and educational freedom. Americans are slowly becoming aware that spiritually and morally, education is basically a religious function, even when it is atheistic, and Christian education is
hardly viable without religious freedom. As Dr. Rushdoony writes:

"Among Nietzche's manuscripts, after his death, was found
a slip of paper on which he had written these words: 'Since
the old God has been abolished, I am prepared to rule the
world.' This is the meaning of humanism's inescapable totalitarianism. Total government is a necessity, and everything in man requires it. If there is no god to provide it,
then man must supply it. . . .

"In the United States, the efforts of federal and state governments to control churches and Christian Schools are the log-

ical results of their humanism. There must be sovereignty and law, and it must be man's, not God's, is their faith. Clearly, we are in the basic religious war, and there can be no compromise nor negotiation in this war. Humanism seeks to abolish the God of Scripture and rule the world."

Who owns our children?

In America, the ultimate aims of humanism can only be achieved through the control of children and their education. The fundamental issue, therefore, is the ownership of children. Do humanists have the right to indoctrinate children in the public schools with humanist values without the knowledge or consent of the parents? On this issue, Dr. Rushdoony writes:

"The first and basic premise of paganism, socialism, and Molech worship is the claim that the state owns the child. The basic premise of the public schools is this claim of ownership, a fact some parents are encountering in the courts. It is the essence of paganism to claim first the lives of the children, then the properties of the people."

There are many cases in which compulsory school attendance laws have been used to deprive parents of their children. The most egregious case I know of is that of Barry Bear, an 18-year-old youth, who has spent the last five years in state custody in Iowa because of truancy. Barry's mother, Anna Bear, is a white woman married to a Native American with whom she has had four sons and a daughter. The family lives on a reservation near Tama. Barry is mildly retarded and has what the public schools like to call "special needs." But like many retarded children, Barry suffers from a variety of ailments, mainly gastro-intestinal. And so, when it came to attending school, Barry was absent a great deal. However, that should not have bothered the school, since Anna Bear taught school for twenty years, was certified, and could teach Barry at home.

The homeschooling family is creating a revolution in American family life.

However, in May 1989 the Iowa Supreme Court ordered that Barry, then 12, be forced to attend school. His parents refused. And so in 1991, after a long court battle, Barry was removed from his home and placed in foster care. Barry has now been in state custody for five years. He's been in four or five foster homes, four or five public schools in which he's learned how to tie his shoelaces but not much else. He is presently at a residential hospital where he is being drugged and has become addicted. This mild, gentle boy has become a violent young adult who wants to go home and be with his parents and brothers and sisters, but the state will not let him go home. He is now their prisoner, and even though he has reached the age of 18 and is beyond compulsory school age, the court refuses to release him. Why? Because they own him, and they want every homeschooler in Iowa to know that they own him and every other child they can get their clutches on.

And we know why. The *Des Moines Register* of Jan. 12, 1989 carried the following small item under the heading of "Statehouse Briefing":

> "Iowa prosecutors are seeking more power to intervene in truancy cases and have suggested law changes that could give county attorneys more tools to use against fundamentalist Christians who want to teach their children at home.

> "Recommendations from the Iowa County Attorneys' Association include a change in the state's juvenile code to add truancy to the list of reasons officials can start proceedings that can lead to removing the child from the home or to terminating the parents' rights to their child."

Thus the humanist state can legally kidnap any child it wants through the compulsory education laws, and keep that child prisoner for as long as it wants. Which means that the issue of Christian liberty can only be resolved in a philosophical confrontation between Christians and the state. I say philosophical confrontation, not a physical confrontation, since the government has shown little restraint in its handling of citizens who disagree with its laws. (The ATF [Bureau of Alcohol, Tobacco and Firearms] called out the U.S. Army with tanks and helicopters and 70 armed agents just to serve the hapless David Koresh with a search warrant for what?—a technical gun violation which would have gotten Koresh maybe 3 months in jail if found guilty.) Which means that you don't confront this crazy government physically if you want to survive. As long as this civil war can be fought in the courts and in the polling booths and by the legal actions of its citizens, there is no reason for physical confrontation.

Recognizing God's sovereignty

Our goal must be the recognition of God's sovereignty over this nation. The principle of God's ownership was implicitly understood by the Founding Fathers who wrote the U.S. Constitution and upheld God's sovereignty over man. George Washington, in his inaugural address in 1789 after being sworn in as first President of the United States under the new Constitution, said:

> "Such being the impression under which I have, in obedience to the public summons, repaired to the present station, it would be peculiarly improper to omit, in this first official act, my fervent supplications to that Almighty Being who rules over the universe, who presides in the councils of nations and whose providential aids can supply every human defect; . . .

> "No people can be bound to acknowledge and adore the Invisible Hand which conducts the affairs of men more than the people of the United States. Every step by which they have advanced to the character of an independent nation seems to have been distinguished by some token of providential agency. . . .

"We ought to be no less persuaded that the propitious smiles of Heaven can never be expected on a nation that disregards the eternal rules of order and right which Heaven itself has ordained; and since the preservation of the sacred fire of liberty and the destiny of the republican model of government are justly considered as deeply, perhaps finally, staked on the experiment."

Thus, it was clearly understood at the very birth of the American republic that God's sovereignty ruled over the United States and that as long as the civil government remained subordinate to God's sovereignty, it was legitimate and thereby supportable by Christians.

The loss of religious liberty

But the introduction of secular, government-owned and -controlled schools and colleges began to erode that basic understanding in the minds of the American people. Statism, the philosophy that the state is the supreme power, slowly absorbed the loyalty of America's academic elite.

Slowly but surely the concept of religious freedom gave way to that of religious toleration. The original concept of religious freedom meant that the state had no jurisdiction over the church, its schools, or its affairs. But the new doctrine of religious toleration meant that the state granted certain privileges to churches and religious schools at its own pleasure; privileges, such as tax exemption, which could be withdrawn at any time "compelling state interest." Dr. Rushdoony writes:

"The fact is that religious liberty is dead and buried; it needs to be resurrected. We cannot begin to cope with our present crisis until we recognize that religious liberty has been replaced with religious toleration. . . .

"We may be able to live under religious toleration, but it will beget all the ancient evils of compromise, hypocrisy, and a purely or largely public religion. It will replace conscience with a state license, and freedom with a state-endowed cell of narrow limits. This is the best that toleration may afford us in the days ahead."

The impact of statism

This basic philosophy of statism and religious toleration has important ramifications for the Christian family. Dr. Rushdoony writes:

"In scripture, the family is the basic institution of society, to whom all the most basic powers are given, save one: the death penalty. (Hence, the death penalty could not be executed on Cain.) The family is man's basic government, his best school, and his best church. . . .

"To review briefly the basic powers which Scripture gives to the family, the first is the control of children. The control of children is the control of the future. This power belongs neither to church nor state, nor to the school, but only to the family. . . .

"Second, power over property is given in Scripture to the family. . . . God gives control of property into the hands of the family, not the state, nor the individual. . . .

"Third, the inheritance in Scripture is exclusively a family power, governed by God's law. . . .

"Fourth, welfare is the responsibility of the family, beginning with the care of its own.

"Fifth, education, a basic power, is given by God to the family as its power and responsibility. The modern state claims the right to control and provide education, and it challenges the powers of the family in this area also. . . .

"Humanistic statism sees control of the child and the family as basic to its drive towards totalitarianism."

The importance of home schooling

I think you can sense now why the homeschooling movement is so important to America during this time of cultural civil war. The means to restore Christian liberty and Constitutional government are limited by the very circumstances of the battlefield. The battlefields of this civil war are to be found in the court houses, the legislatures, the media, and most important of all, in the actions that citizens can take to further the cause of freedom and Godly government.

The home is a safe haven for the children in a world awash with drugs, sexually transmitted diseases, violence, and moral corruption.

One of the most important actions families can take is to remove their children from the government schools and homeschool them. By now about a million families have made that choice, and their actions have had an accumulative effect on American life that is only now beginning to be felt.

While the government asserts implicitly in court decisions here and there that it owns the children, it cannot say so explicitly to the public at large for fear of provoking a violent reaction. And so school districts subtly assert the state-ownership principle by requiring parents to request permission to homeschool and requiring homeschooled children to be tested. Some school districts require more and some less, depending on the disposition of the superintendent. But in some districts, where humanist superintendents refuse to acknowledge parents' rights and impose onerous conditions for homeschooling, parents have had to fight in court to defend their God-given right to educate their children as they see fit.

Despite the obstacles involved, the withdrawal of children from the humanist state system is significant because it means that those children will be free from statist, humanist, indoctrination. It means that the Christian family will be free to raise their children in a Godly way, in a way that conforms with the principles and values of the founding fathers. These are the children who will mold America's future and restore God's sovereignty over our government.

Home schooling and the Christian family

What is also important is what the homeschool movement is doing for the Christian family. Homeschoolers are rediscovering the benefits and joys and blessings of family life. For it is in the family that love for one another and love of God is nurtured. The very act of educating one's own children is a Godly act called for in Deuteronomy [a book of Jewish and Christian Scripture]. And therefore, it brings the Christian family in obedience to God's law and reestablishes the family as a unit governed under God, equal to the civil government. American civil government was never meant to usurp, replace or negate family government.

The civil government must respect family government for they both derive their legitimacy from the same divine source. But today's civil government has done all in its power to make the family totally subordinate to the state by taking control of the children through compulsory attendance laws and using state social agencies to undermine the integrity of the family.

It is true that dysfunctional families pose a problem for society. But in the past it was the church or private agencies that dealt with such problems. Today, when the state takes control over a family, it plays the role of God. Social workers place children in foster homes that sometimes turn out to be worse than the homes they were taken from. And, of course, drug addiction and unwed teenage motherhood has exacerbated the dysfunctional family problem. Detached from God, these people become the victims of their own innate depravity.

But we should not lose our freedoms, and parents should not lose their rights simply because a portion of the population acts self-destructively. We cannot expect the drug addicts and unwed teenage mothers on welfare to save our country. Nor should we let them prevent us from doing what has to be done to restore America as a nation under God.

And so, the homeschool family is on the frontline of this civil war, and we can only win this long, drawn-out war one family at a time. The quiet revolution is taking place right under the very noses of the humanists, and there isn't much they can do about it.

The home schooling moral revolution

Meanwhile, the homeschooling family is creating a revolution in American family life. The Christian family that lives in obedience to God sets a standard of morality that will stay with their children for the rest of their lives. That even some homeschooled children may go astray is inevitable, knowing what we do about human nature. But the vast majority are becoming the kind of citizens we can all be proud of.

And so, the reconstruction of the American family is one of the great benefits of the homeschool movement. The homeschooling family creates a generation bridge instead of a generation gap. Parents can pass on to their children their spiritual and moral values, thereby creating family continuity into several generations.

Homeschooled children learn to respect their parents' intelligence, and the parents, who know their children better than any stranger could, enjoy teaching their children. I myself have no children, but I've always thought that one of the greatest pleasures of parenthood must be the act of instructing one's own children in all that is good and valuable, showing them what a wonderful world they were born in, what a wonderful God we have that has given us life and inspired our founding fathers to create a country of such great freedom. What a joy it is to introduce a child to poetry, or great music and art, or the wonders of nature, or to playful puppies and kittens, or to horseback riding, swimming, ice-skating, and heaven knows what else.

The academic and social benefits

Did you know that homeschoolers learn better than public schoolers? Wherever homeschoolers have taken standardized achievement tests, they've come out ahead of the public schoolers. Why? Because the home is a better place to learn than a school. One-on-one teaching is more effective than the classroom. Also, at home the preschoolers learn from their older siblings. They can't help but learn because they hear it and see it all around them.

I look forward to the day when the public schools will be virtually empty not because we have abolished public education but because the parents . . . will have abandoned it.

And did you know that homeschooling parents learn more than their children? Quite an interesting phenomenon. Many parents don't realize that when they begin teaching their children math or grammar or history or a foreign language they are also learning these subjects. In fact, because homeschoolers generally use phonics to teach their children to read, they improve their own reading skills by learning the phonics they didn't have when they were in school. Most of today's young home-schooling parents were taught to read by the Dick-and-Jane look-say method and were deprived of the kind of intensive phonics necessary to become a good reader. Thus, learning phonics through teaching it to their children has been enormously beneficial.

Another important benefit of homeschooling is that the home is a safe haven for the children in a world awash with drugs, sexually transmitted diseases, violence, and moral corruption. Children need all the protection they can get. If you want a child to get involved with drugs, send him or her to a public school, the principle market place for drugs in America. That's where peer pressure is used to hook a child. If you want your child to become suicidal, just give him a good dose of death education. If you want your child to become sexually active, just give him or her explicit sex education beginning in kindergarten with instructions on how to use a condom. If you want your child to lose his religious faith, just subject him to endless lessons about evolution, critical thinking—which means criticizing your folks and your religion. If you want your child to start putting rings through his nose and safety pins in his eyebrows or navel, send him to a public school where his peers will persuade him of the beauties of self mutilation.

Homeschooling provides healthful socialization, not the negative kind you get in the public school. In homeschooling, brothers and sisters get to know one another very well and they become lifelong friends. In the public school, brothers and sisters go their separate ways, bonding with their own clique of friends, engaging in mischievous behavior, drinking, smoking, dating, getting high, listening to acid rock music, having sex. Homeschooled kids get to know other homeschooled kids. Their Christian code of morals determines their behavior. They believe in courtship, not dating. They are future oriented, planning to have long, healthful, productive lives. The public school teenager lives for the moment, the thrill, the party. Otherwise, they are bored, hanging out at malls or parking lots, killing time before going home to surly parents. "Where'd you go?" "Nowhere." "What did'ya do?" "Nothing."

But perhaps the greatest dividend that homeschoolers enjoy is the taking back and mastery of their own time. Time is one of the most precious commodities a family has, and the more time a family can devote to its own improvement and enjoyment, the better it is for all of its members. Public schools squander the best time in a family's life. They rob the family of the time that could be spent together, learning, playing, and creating. The state wants that time in order to do its work of indoctrination. But that time belongs to your family.

Another development among homeschoolers is their political awakening. They know that they must get more God-fearing men in the Congress and state legislatures. They made quite a difference in the elections of November 1994. You must become politically active and stay politically active for the other side would like nothing better than to get politicians in power who will vote to make homeschooling illegal.

I think you get the gist of what I am driving at. You are very important to America's future, more important than you will ever know. You are the revolutionaries doing God's work, one family at a time. I like to look at our humanist education system as a big hour-glass. Each grain of sand is a child, and every second of that hour several grains of sand fall through the tiny hole separating the top from the bottom. Eventually the top will be empty. How long it will take, no one knows. But I look forward to the day when the public schools will be virtually empty not because we have abolished public education but because the parents for the most part will have abandoned it. Yes, there will be those who will send their children to the public schools out of ignorance, or indifference, or a misguided loyalty to an institution that no longer works. But the taxpayers may decide that keeping the public schools open for that diminished group is uneconomical and simply provide the families with tuition to attend private schools. Who knows, we may yet see such a day in the not too distant future.

13

Home-Schooled Students May Fail to Learn America's Cultural Heritage

Martha de Acosta

Martha de Acosta is the director of education and training programs at the Milton S. Eisenhower Foundation, a nonprofit organization that studies and reports on inner cities.

While parents may be able to promote academic success or convey a personal value system through home schooling, they may fail to convey America's cultural heritage or teach democratic ideals. In fact, these parents may be limiting their children's access to new ideas through social isolation. Their children may never learn to value or interact with people from different backgrounds, a necessary element in a racially and ethnically diverse country like the United States. The best way for parents to improve their children's education is to enroll them in public school and stay actively involved in their education.

M any parents choose home schooling because they want to transmit their beliefs and values to their children. They find some of the values taught at school objectionable.

Other parents primarily want to enhance their children's academic performance.

Studies conducted by home schooling advocates claim that both of these goals are met successfully by home schooling. Parents report that they feel they have passed on their beliefs to their children, and data on test scores indicates that, as a group, home-schooled children's performance is above average on standardized tests.

Cultural heritage must be introduced

An important shortcoming of home schooling, however, is the inability to meet crucial aspects of education's societal goals, namely, the transmission of our cultural heritage and children's socialization into our modern, democratic society.

Families have a right to teach their beliefs and values to their children and protect them from danger. Parents who teach their children at home, however, take on the additional challenge of introducing their children to our cultural heritage. In a scientifically and technologically advanced, democratic society, education must introduce its citizens to the current state of knowledge, prepare them to thoughtfully assess the soundness of different arguments and views and, when necessary, choose among them. Those families who choose home schooling to create a shield around their world view may be restricting their children's access to a broad range of ideas and passing on a narrow cultural legacy.

The social isolation of home-schooled children is another concern about this alternative form of education. While there is evidence that home-schooled children have no problem playing and interacting with other children, there is no data indicating that their interaction extends beyond the limited circles in which their families move. Citizens' ability to understand, respect and interact with people with views and backgrounds different from their own is one of the conditions for our racially, ethnically and culturally diverse society to prosper and not become Balkanized [to break up into smaller, often hostile groups].

Parental involvement is crucial

The critical variable in accomplishing student academic success is parent involvement. More than 30 years of research show that family involvement in children's education has strong positive effects on academic achievement and children's attitudes and behaviors. Although, as a group, children who are home-schooled perform well academically, this important accomplishment is not unique to home schooling. As a group, children who regularly attend school and whose parents are involved in their schooling also outperform their peers.

Concerned citizens, including home-schooling parents, have made valid criticisms about schools. Schools do need to change their pedagogy and curriculum to adapt to social and technological trends and provide safe and stimulating learning environments. Even so, schools remain a viable way of teaching children how to become members of the larger community. Parents who are thinking of home schooling because they want to strongly influence their children's education should consider what they could gain by opting to partner with school and community educators instead. Parent involvement in their children's schooling offers the advantages that close relationships between parents and children give home-schooled children. At the same time, parent involvement in schooling gives children the added advantages that attending school provides, including transmission of our cultural heritage through a full range of curricular offerings and interaction with many and diverse peers.

14

Cooperation Between Public Schools and Home-Schooling Parents Is Needed

Michael H. Romanowski

Michael H. Romanowski is an associate professor in the Department of Education at Ohio Northern University.

Home schooling has become a legitimate educational method in the United States, appealing to a diverse demographic. However, an antagonistic and, therefore, damaging relationship exists between home-schooling parents who feel threatened by state involvement and educators who misunderstand the reasons for home schooling. Each side must develop more positive views of the other and enter into dialogues that can lead to a more enriched learning environment for all children.

Once considered an anomaly in American education, home schooling has become an increasingly popular alternative to both public and private schools in today's culture, an estimated 1,200,000 to 1,700,000 U.S. K–2 students currently being home-schooled. This spectacular growth not only testifies to parental demand for less institutionalized options for their children's education, but has also established home schooling as a significant and legitimate force in the American educational landscape.

One of the more fascinating aspects of the home-school movement is its appeal to a demographic diversity that includes virtually all races, religions, socioeconomic groups, and political viewpoints. There are conservatives who consider public education too liberal, liberals who consider it too conservative, and those who are driven by religious convictions.

Despite its growth, however, home schooling is not without problems and difficulties. In particular, its relationship with public schools is often tense, due partly to lack of understanding by public school educators of why parents choose to home-school their children. This results in the "us versus them" mentality that often governs relationships between professional educators and home-school parents. Both need to rethink their roles and build partnerships that will benefit children wherever they are taught.

Motivations for home schooling

Although parents choose to home-school their children for many reasons, they might be categorized as ideologues and pedagogues. Ideologues have specific beliefs, values, and skills they want their children to learn and embrace. Convinced these things are not being adequately taught in public school, they opt for home schooling.

The ideologues' motivation is essentially religion-based, believing public schools have a secular humanist philosophy without strong Christian values. They have a strong concern for their children's moral, ethical, and spiritual development, and feel public schools fail to take religion seriously. For these parents, religious beliefs and the education of their children are inextricably intertwined.

Pedagogues prefer to teach their children at home primarily because they feel it will benefit their children's education. They are less concerned with public education content than with their conviction that whatever public schools teach, they don't teach well. Often, these parents have turned to home schooling after having experienced or observed children suffering emotionally and/or academically in public schools.

Pedagogues also feel schools are often unwilling or unable to serve children with unique learning styles or scholarly needs. They challenge the power of public schools to sort, select, and label their children based on what they see as a limited measure of their ability. This leads them to believe that breaking from the traditional formal teaching model will lead to improved understanding and learning in their children.

The most common—and most damaging—conflict between public school educators and parents who opt to home-school is the "us versus them" attitude grounded in their limited and often negative experiences with each other. Home-school parents are stereotyped as loners who do not care about the opinions of others, as people who are withdrawn from society and want to shelter their children from the "evil" of public schools. They are often viewed as arrogant because they express their view that public schools aren't good enough for their children.

The "us versus them" mentality creates an atmosphere of distrust that can produce negative results.

Many public school teachers and principals view home schooling as a serious threat and take offense at what they regard as personal attacks on their profession and abilities. They see home educators as professionally and academically inferior and accuse home schooling of lacking in social development, classroom-provided stimulation of ideas, and academic and social competition.

Although there may be some truth in these stereotypes, the "us versus them" mentality creates an atmosphere of distrust that can produce negative results. First, these opposing perspectives inhibit any formal co-operation between home and public schools. Second, the tension and un-easiness between home schoolers and public educators discourages any formal or informal dialogues, discussions, or sharing of ideas between them. In the long run, students lose, because shared information might improve learning and academic success in both educational settings.

For this to change, public school educators and home-schooling parents must review and rethink their views of education and their roles in the education process. How can they overcome the "us versus them" barrier?

How home-schoolers can change. First, home-school parents must begin to move from negative views of public schools and start to perceive the important, essential role of U.S. public education. They must develop an understanding of the responsibilities public schools bear and view themselves not as self-contained entitles, but as part of a larger educational system deserving their support. This support can range from monetary donations to volunteering. It is key for home-school parents to get involved with their public schools because home educators who feel connected to their schools support them more fully. This understanding and support are also needed because all citizens benefit from public education.

Public educators should join home-schoolers in mutually beneficial relationships that improve chances for the academic success of both public school and home-school children.

How public-school educators can change. Principals and teachers must also begin to transform negative views of home schooling and parents who choose it, recognizing that parents have the primary responsibility for educating their children, and that parents, the school, and the community must work together to maximize every child's potential. Rather than questioning motives and feeling threatened when families home-school, public-school educators should aid those families wherever possible. The public school's responsibility is not only to students in the schoolhouse, but to all students in the community.

By working with rather than against home-schoolers, public schools can benefit from new approaches to parent involvement, individualized instruction, use of technology in learning, one-on-one tutoring, distance learning, and child-initiated learning. Other possible areas might involve the effects of different learning environments on student achievement and the impact of varied curricula on student learning.

Evidence shows most home schoolers do very well on achievement tests, often outperforming their public school peers. Since proficiency testing often drives public education, public schools should be particularly interested in why home-schooled children perform well on these tests, and how this knowledge could be used by public-school teachers to help students improve their scores. But for home schooling to make these contributions to public education, there must be a climate of mutual understanding and respect.

Building a working relationship. Instead of viewing themselves as competitors, the public school and home school should be seen as complementing each other. Both have their place and purpose in the educational process of a free society. Here important, mutual recognition and respect can be the basis for developing a productive relationship.

Despite a more favorable legal climate for home schooling now than in earlier years, allowing home-school families to remain completely removed from public education, many such families want to build positive working relationships with their public schools. A recent study in Virginia revealed that most home-schooling parents want such relationships with local public schools, and that they would welcome assistance in the form of classes, inservices, use of school facilities and materials, and curriculum information.

Building on the relationship

Here are some ways to begin building a home school–public school relationship:

Exchange ideas. This is especially important to home schoolers, many of whom depend on a home-school network for ideas and support. Both public-school teachers and home-school parents could benefit from a formal system enabling them to engage in pedagogical dialogue. This dialogue could take forms ranging from e-mailing specific questions and answers on particular issues to sharing inservice training, curriculum information, and school facilities with home-school parents. I know of one public school teacher who even offered to conduct a special parents' night for homeschool parents to discuss issues relevant to their children's education.

Offer dual enrollment, where home-schooled students are able to enroll in their school district for academic or instructional programs, participate in any district-offered extracurricular activity, and use the services of the appropriate area education agency. In practice, home-schooled students usually attend public-school "specials," such as art, music, physical education, chorus, and band. Dual enrollment also allows them to participate in sports, have access to district textbooks and resources, participate in standardized testing, and take enrichment classes.

While it seems obvious that home schooling would benefit most from this arrangement, public schools also benefit in terms of community and financial support. For example, school districts in Iowa can receive state aid for home-schooled children who choose to be part of their school community. Perhaps even more important are the intangible benefits that may accrue as home educators develop a connection with their schools and begin to more fully appreciate and support them.

Provide a home-school liaison. Ideally, public schools could designate a coordinator to work with home-school families who desire a connection to public education. At the minimum, this individual could help home-school parents understand and conform to state education requirements. But the liaison could also help develop appropriate programs and guidelines meeting the needs of both public and home schools.

The liaison role must not be perceived as an attempt to control home schooling. This can be avoided if the liaison is selected by a group that includes both public school educators and home-schoolers. Because the consensus among home-schoolers is that each family should make its own decisions about education, religion, and lifestyle, a liaison's sole purpose should be to help define and satisfy the educational needs of each home-schooled child.

Because the great majority of parents have neither the desire nor resources for home schooling, it should not be viewed as a threat to public education. Public educators should join home-schoolers in mutually beneficial relationships that improve chances for the academic success of both public school and home-school children. When public schools work closely with home-school families, they demonstrate that their goal is to help every child reach his or her educational goals. This is the essence of a truly democratic educational system.

15

Self-Directed Learning Prepares Children for Adulthood

Kate Tsubata

Kate Tsubata is a freelance writer who home schools her three children.

Student desire and effort are the impetus behind home-school learning, making parental background insignificant. Students, therefore, are not teacher-dependent. Once students realize that they can understand material on their own, they take responsibility for their own learning, initiating and following through on educational projects. As a result, home schooling allows children to practice adult behavior.

Each month, my children send their completed assignments to the correspondence school in which they are enrolled. A few weeks later, we receive a transcript of their marks on those assignments and their overall grade for the period.

Before sending their work, we make a photocopy of their papers to keep for our records and to use to check their work. This morning, while I reviewed their papers for the past month, I noticed how many times their work reflected some dialogue between me and them. Several times a day, we discuss their work and questions they may have or we brainstorm on a certain topic. Sometimes the children initiate this interaction, and sometimes I do.

These conversations may be about biology or weather patterns, psychology or the factoring of polynomials. I often don't know the exact information that is under study. We just work it out together, going back to the examples, checking the textbook for clarification and arriving at some conclusion.

Still, I often am surprised by the final product. All those pages of math proofs and problems—who accomplished all that? Who told the children how to interpret that poem or write that essay?

To be totally honest, I must admit I have very little to do with it. My children study and do their work pretty much independently. They don't learn because I am a great teacher; they learn because they want to learn, and they work hard at it. In other words, the secret ingredient that allows home-schooling to work is the students' desire and effort.

A parent's background is unimportant

This explains a lot. I have noticed that home-schooled children learn well despite the gaps in their parents' education or their parents' lack of professional teaching experience. Some folks have said to me, "Well, you have a lot of teaching experience, and so does your husband. It's natural that you can home-school your children. But how about families in which the parent doesn't have that experience? Do you think they can do a good job?"

Home-schoolers outperform their counterparts regardless of the parents' educational background or teaching experience.

If parents were the key factor in the learning process, perhaps not. But from every report I have encountered, home-schoolers outperform their counterparts regardless of the parents' educational background or teaching experience. This also is true of children using a wide variety of curricula and methods. Why is this? Is it that the children are all geniuses? Or is it that they are simply more able to learn?

Home-schoolers learn independently

The fact is, most home-schoolers are not very teacher-dependent. By that I mean they have discovered they are the ones who are doing the learning, and it is up to them to master the material. At some point along the line, every home-schooled student starts making certain realizations:
- "This material is understandable. I can get it."
- "It's interesting to learn."
- "I can choose how and when I want to learn."
- "Learning this will benefit me."
- "I actually enjoy mastering new information."

From that point, the student begins to take personal responsibility for his or her own education. The children exert their own effort to learn. They control their own schedules. They challenge themselves, set their own deadlines and take pride in the product.

This is such a far cry from supposedly "normal" schooling that most people can't imagine it. Students are supposed to hate books, discipline and challenges. Teachers are supposed to have to lay down the law, enforce the discipline, punish the lazy and contentious and reward the achievers.

The classroom is seen as a competitive marketplace where some are winners and others are losers. Some children are "smart," or "hard-working." Others aren't and must suffer the consequences. Children learn through "the school of hard knocks."

Self-directed learning is natural

The idea of students actually initiating and following through on their own learning seems like nonsense. "Perhaps for a mature college student, or a post-graduate student, learning can be a self-initiated process, but not for young people," is the common thinking.

Yet elementary-age home-schoolers do this quite naturally. Older students often expand this self-initiative into hobby and career-related decisions. They may take a part-time job or an apprenticeship, go on trips or develop nonacademic skills such as computer expertise or talents in the arts.

Recently, my husband and I attended a dinner-theater performance. One of the main roles was played by a 14-year-old boy. His acting was excellent—far better than what most high school or college students can achieve. It turns out he and his three siblings are home-schooled. His mom told us it was his idea to try acting. He manages eight performances a week along with his schoolwork, and he loves the demands of this schedule.

How many eighth-graders would have the self-confidence to try out for such a production, much less balance all that work with a full academic schedule? Somehow, having been home-schooled, this boy is comfortable with envisioning a goal, setting a course of action, carrying it out and being happy with the results.

Test scores aside, this is a tremendous indicator in itself of the value of home-schooling in preparing children for success in their adult endeavors. They are forming important habits that they will carry with them throughout their lives. What's more, that is a lesson they are teaching themselves.

16

Home-Schooled Students Excel in College

Christopher J. Klicka

Christopher J. Klicka is senior counsel of the Home School Legal Defense Association.

Home-schooled students perform well on standardized tests for college entrance and have gained entrance to most colleges. Many colleges report that, once enrolled, home-schooled students perform as well as or better than public school students. Christian colleges, in particular, pursue home-schooled students because they generally have a Christian background. Since more and more colleges recognize the abilities of home-schooled children, these students should not be required to take special standardized exams. In addition, colleges should be flexible in terms of acceptance materials and the submission of letters of recommendation.

Are well-rounded, talented, even academically excellent students encountering cumbersome technical difficulties when they apply at your college or university? [In June 1996], a 16-year-old in Texas made a perfect SAT score. A student in Maryland came within 10 points of perfection, but restrictive admission requirements may cause trouble for them—they are both home educated.

The standardized test results of over 16,000 home educated children, grades K–12, were analyzed in 1994 by researcher Dr. Brian Ray. He found the nationwide grand mean in reading for home schoolers is at the 79th percentile; for language and math, the 73rd percentile. This ranking means home educated students perform better than approximately 77% of the sample population on whom the test was normed. Nearly 80% of home schooled children achieve individual scores above the national average and 54.7% of the 16,000 home schoolers achieved individual scores in the top quarter of the population, more than double the number of conventional school students who score in the top quarter.

The current estimate of home educated students in the United States is 1.23 million to 2 million and growing. Every year a significant portion of these students seek higher education. Individualized training with its creative alternatives cannot be measured accurately by traditional transcripts. Grades are unnecessary and class rank is irrelevant. So how are admissions officers supposed to deal with these unusual cases?

The 1996 survey of admission policies

This fall the National Center for Home Education (NCHE) conducted a nation-wide college survey; a sampling of the home school admission policies in all fifty states. Only 44% had verbal or written policies for home school applicants. NCHE's liberal definition of "policy" includes colleges that take into account home schoolers' unique capabilities and circumstances. Nevertheless, 96% of the colleges polled had at least one and sometimes over 200 home educated students enrolled at their college. Course descriptions or portfolios are accepted in lieu of an accredited diploma or GED by 93% of the schools polled. Several colleges had home schoolers excelling in their honors programs.

On May 10, 1994, the *Wall Street Journal* reported:

> Many colleges now routinely accept home-schooled students, who typically present "portfolios" of their work instead of transcripts. Each year Harvard University takes up to 10 applicants who have had some home schooling. "In general, those kids do just fine," says David Illingworth, senior admissions officer. He adds that the number of applications and inquiries from home schoolers is "definitely increasing."

A positive college experience

The survey of over 60 colleges and universities in all fifty states conducted by the National Center for Home Education revealed the following anecdotal accounts of home schoolers in college:

A Harvard University admissions officer said most of their home educated students "have done very well. They usually are very motivated in what they do." Results of the SAT and SAT II, an essay, an interview, and a letter of recommendation are the main requirements for home educated applicants. "[Transcripts are] irrelevant because a transcript is basically a comparison to other students in the school."

In addition to Harvard, prominent schools like Yale, Princeton, Texas A&M, Brown University, the Carnegie Mellon Institute, the Universities of Arizona, Maryland, Virginia, Hawaii and many others all have flexible transcript criteria, accept parental evaluations, and do not require any accreditation or a General Equivalency Diploma (GED). At Kansas State University and others like Lipscomb University and Middlebury College transcripts are optional.

Birmingham-Southern College had only one home school applicant this year, but the admissions officer said the college "would be glad to have many more just like him!"

Roughly 50 home schoolers attend the University of Montana. "The home schoolers in this state seem to be up to date and well organized. We even have home schoolers in our honors programs. I know of one student for sure. She is one of our top students," remarked one admissions official.

Bruce Walker at the University of Delaware said one home educated student who "had an exceptional SAT score was invited to be considered for a full ride scholarship!"

"Home schooling is becoming more and more prevalent," said Mark Wheeler of Boise State University. "We're all trying to work together." Pennsylvania State University had 20 home school applicants in 1995, double the previous year. They prefer a portfolio with as much information as possible, including extracurricular activities that demonstrate leadership. "Home schoolers show strongly in that," said the admissions officer for Penn State.

Home schoolers . . . tend to exhibit "a strong work ethic" and have high moral values which contribute to their success in college.

Lewis and Clark College has a method of application called the "Portfolio Path" where a student can bypass standardized tests and instead be "reviewed on a myriad of things that would point to, and measure academic performance." The Universities of Minnesota and Mississippi also look at the all-around abilities demonstrated in a home schooler's portfolio. University of Kentucky home school applicants "have to provide a portfolio of what they have done throughout their high school years" that is "creative and informative." A UK admissions officer also said, "Our home schoolers (about 50) tend to be very bright, and have scored very high on standardized tests."

The Dartmouth College admissions officer explained, "The applications I've come across are outstanding. Home schoolers have a distinct advantage because of the individualized instruction they have received."

University of Alaska/Fairbanks has had over 300 home educated students in the last few years, several of which were in their honors program. The program director, Mary Dicicco commented, "They have been wonderful students on the whole. Tess was a marvelous student!"

Staff from Geneva College (PA) and Belhaven College (MS) are actively recruiting home schoolers by going to home school conferences and book fairs to talk to parents and students about admissions.

"Home schoolers have to work harder thereby increasing student productivity," Jeff Lantis said of the 75–90 home schoolers at Hillsdale College (MI). "Home schoolers are consistently among our top students, in fact home schoolers have won our distinct Honors Program the last three years in a row. We tend to look very favorably upon home schoolers applying to our college."

USA Today reported on October 28, 1996, that the University of North Carolina-Chapel Hill's dean of admissions, James Walters,. has enrolled about 20 home educated students, all of which "are performing above average academically."

A letter sent in 1990 to home school leaders in Massachusetts from George A. Schiller, Jr., Director of Admissions at Boston University is another example of the recognition institutions of higher learning are showing home schoolers' academic achievements:

"Boston University welcomes applications from home schooled students. We believe students educated at home possess the passion for knowledge, the independence, and the self-reliance that enable them to excel in our intellectually challenging programs of study."

How are home schoolers scoring on college entrance exams?

We knew home schoolers on average, do better on national standardized achievement tests for the elementary and secondary grade levels. Now recent statistics released find that home schoolers, on average, are above the national average on their ACT scores.

The ACT High School Profile Report of the home school graduating class of 1996, which comprised 2,369 students, the students on average scored 22.5. In 1997, another profile report was made of the results of 1,926 home school graduates and found that home schoolers maintained the average of 22.5.

This is higher than the national average of 20.9 in 1996 and 21.0 in 1997. The perfect score for the ACT is 36.

The 1996 ACT results showed that in English, home schoolers scored 22.5 compared to the national average of 20.3. In math, home schoolers scored 19.2 compared to the national average of 20.2. In reading, home schoolers outshone their public school counterparts 24.1 to 21.3. In science, home schoolers scored 21.9 compared to 21.1.

The conclusion is obvious: home schooling works!

Home schoolers in college

The *U.S. News & World Report* reported on December 9, 1991, that an "estimated 50 percent of home-schooled students attend college, about the same rate as their public-school counterparts." How are home schoolers performing in college? "[A]s well as, if not better than, their conventionally educated counterparts," was the report from a study conducted through Bob Jones University (SC).

Paulo de Oliveira, Ed.D., Dr. Timothy Watson, and Dr. Joe Sutton [of the National Home Education Research Institute] studied 789 students and discovered that college freshmen who had completed their entire high school education in a home school had a "slightly higher overall . . . critical thinking score" than students educated in public or private schools. This offers "strong validation that home education is a viable and effective educational alternative."

Rhonda Galloway, Ed.D., joined Dr. Sutton to compare college aptitude and found that "home schooled students demonstrate similar academic preparedness [and] achievement in college as students who have attended conventional schools." They concluded that, consistent with the success of home schoolers at the elementary and secondary levels, "home schooled students can perform adequately in the different, and more advanced, academic setting of college-level study."

Many Christian colleges are rushing to obtain more home school applicants because they find the home schooled student generally has a strong Christian foundation and excels academically. For instance, an investigation conducted in the fall of 1994 by Mike Mitchell, dean of enrollment management of Oral Roberts University (OK) discovered that 212 home schooled students were enrolled at ORU which is about 10% of the student body. The average home schooler had an above average ACT score of 24.0 and SAT score of 1005. The study showed that although home schoolers had virtually the same ACT/SAT average as the ORU student body, they had a statistically higher cumulative GPA at ORU. The average ORU GPA is 2.76 while the average ORU home schooler GPA is 3.02.

Furthermore the study revealed that 88% of ORU home schooled students were involved in one or more outreach ministries. Many of the home schoolers serve as Chaplains in the dorms and virtually all embrace the Honor Code as an already adopted way of life. In addition, over 90% of ORU home schoolers are involved in intramural sports and nearly 80% are involved in various campus clubs and organizations. Home schoolers are active in all areas of college life.

Requiring only home school students to take [SAT II] tests, in addition to the SAT, is discriminatory.

On October 10, 1997, the results of a four-year study was released by Drs. Rhonda Galloway and Joe Sutton. The purpose of conducting the study was to find out how home schoolers fared in the college setting as compared to Christian and public school graduates. The study tracked 180 students, 60 graduates from home schooling, public school, and Christian school. Five success indicators were used in the study: Academic, Cognitive, Spiritual, Affective-Social, and Psychomotor.

Galloway and Sutton found that in every success category except psychomotor, the home school graduates excelled above the other students. Out of 12 academic indicators, the home schoolers ranked first in 10. Out of 11 spiritual indicators, home schoolers ranked first in seven. In cognitive skills, home schoolers ranked first in 17 of the 23 indicators. Out of 63 total indicators, home schoolers ranked first in 42.

Scholarships and athletic eligibility

As a result of the above study, Oral Roberts University created a unique Home School College Preparatory Program and established a $6,000 scholarship especially for home school graduates, above and beyond all other financial aid.

Eager to attract these bright young students, other colleges are developing Home School Scholarships. Belhaven College grants $1,000 a year to qualified home educated students. Nyack College (NY) says their "experience with home schoolers has been a positive one" and awards up to $12,000 to home schoolers. Liberty University (VA) recognizes the "hard work, dedication, and self-motivation behind your success in home education" and also extends "a $12,000 scholarship."

According to the *Chronicle of Higher Education,* June 7, 1996, the National Association of Intercollegiate Athletics and the National Christian College Athletic Association both have guidelines for home schoolers. This year, the National Collegiate Athletic Association (NCAA) drew up new "guidelines to help standardize eligibility for home-schooled athletes. According to the guidelines, home-schooled athletes who have sufficiently high standardized-test scores and proof that they took at least 13 courses that meet the association's core-course standards may be automatically awarded freshman eligibility." An NCAA spokeswoman said that from 1988 to 1993, as many as 10 home-taught athletes applied for waivers each year. "In each of the past three years," she said, "that number has grown to more than 20."

How are colleges recruiting home schoolers?

- by attending state home school conventions and making specialized presentations,
- developing college preparatory programs targeted at home schoolers,
- sponsoring on-campus recruitment activities and visitation opportunities,
- communicating regularly with state-wide home school organizations,
- joining in on home school radio network broadcasts,
- conducting workshops for home schoolers and their parents to help them plan for college admission (like Penn State's Home Schooling High Schoolers Conference),
- offering special scholarships,
- and advertising in brochures and home school publications like *Teaching Home, Practical Home Schooling, Home Schooling Today,* and other magazines.

National Center for Home Education recommendations

Home educated high school graduates offer an academically and socially creative background. Home schoolers also tend to exhibit "a strong work ethic" and have high moral values which contribute to their success in college. More and more colleges and universities are recognizing their unique capabilities and circumstances. In light of the proven success of home education at the elementary, secondary, and post-secondary levels, we recommend colleges adopt specific written home school admission policies which reflect the following:

1. Should home educated applicants be required to submit an accredited diploma or GED? No, accreditation does nothing to measure a student's knowledge or what he was taught, it only reflects *where* he was taught. A GED carries with it the stigma of being a high school drop-out. Home schoolers are not drop-outs, but talented, conscientious students who have completed their high school education. They should not be treated as drop-outs by being required to obtain a GED.

2. If a transcript is required, colleges should have flexible guidelines for records and documentation of the basic credit hours for high school completion. Some colleges supply home schoolers with a

"Home School Credit Evaluation Form" that may be completed in lieu of a transcript.

3. As the primary instructors, parents should be recognized as capable of evaluating their student's academic competence for letters of recommendation. Schools frequently ask for an additional evaluation from someone outside the home.

4. SAT/ACT scores and portfolios or performance-based assessments provide schools with a solid basis for admission. Like most colleges, the University of Missouri-Columbia relies heavily on test results and the dozen or so home schoolers they have in every freshman class "tend to have excellent test score results." In addition, UMC emphasized a GPA is "not a factor in admitting home schoolers."

5. Mandatory SAT II testing in specific subjects is an unnecessary road block. Requiring only home school students to take these tests, in addition to the SAT, is discriminatory. Colleges will discourage home schoolers from seeking admission by holding them to this unreasonable standard. SAT/ACT testing is more than enough to show academic levels.

6. A bibliography of high school literature and an essay are two admission criteria for accurately evaluating a student's exposure and thinking skills. "These home schoolers write fabulous essays!" said Emory University. "Very creative!"

7. Extracurricular activities and interviews are two of the best ways to focus on overall student proficiency and leadership qualities.

Organizations to Contact

The editors have compiled the following list of organizations concerned with the issues debated in this book. The descriptions are derived from materials provided by the organizations. All have publications or information available for interested readers. The list was compiled on the date of publication of the present volume; names, addresses, phone and fax numbers, and e-mail addresses may change. Be aware that many organizations take several weeks or longer to respond to inquiries, so allow as much time as possible.

American Homeschool Association (AHA)
P.O. Box 3142, Palmer, AK 99645
(800) 236-3278
e-mail: aha@americanhomeschoolassociation.org
website: www.americanhomeschoolassociation.org

The AHA is an organization created to network home schoolers on a national level. Current AHA services include an online news and discussion list which provides news, information, and resources for home-schooling families.

Education Law Association (ELA)
300 College Park-0528, Dayton, OH 45469
(937) 229-3589 • fax: (937) 229-3845
e-mail: ela@udayton.edu • website: www.educationlaw.org

The ELA is a nonprofit, nonadvocacy organization that promotes interest in and understanding of the legal framework of education and the rights of students, parents, school boards, and school employees. It supports scholarly research through its newsletters, the *ELA Notes* and the *School Law Reporter*, as well as presentations at conferences, seminars, and professional forums.

Home School Legal Defense Association (HSLDA)
P.O. Box 3000, Purcellville, VA 20134
(540) 338-5600 • fax: (540) 338-2733
e-mail: info@hslda.org • website: www.hslda.org

HSLDA is a Christian organization of home-schooling families. The association's goal is to protect the rights and freedoms of home schoolers of all faiths. It supports home-schooling families by negotiating with local officials, serving as an advocate in court proceedings, monitoring federal legislation, and fighting any proposed laws seen as harmful. The HSLDA produces the *Home School Heartbeat*, a two-minute daily radio program, and publishes *The Home School Court Report*.

National Black Home Educators Resource Association (NBHERA)
6943 Stoneview Ave., Baker, LA 70714
(225) 778-0169 • fax: (225) 774-4114
e-mail: nbhera@internet8.net • website: www.christianity.com/nbhera

NBHERA offers services and information on getting started in home education, networking with national/local organizations, pairing new home-school families with veteran families, and selecting teaching materials and curriculum. NBHERA also provides its members with a quarterly newsletter.

National Center for Education Statistics (NCES)
1990 K St. NW, Washington, DC 20006
(202) 502-7300
website: http://nces.ed.gov

NCES is the primary federal entity for collecting and analyzing data that are related to education in the United States and other countries. The center organizes training seminars, holds conferences, and publishes its findings in reports and in its publications, including the *Education Statistics Quarterly* and the *Digest of Education Statistics*.

National Education Association (NEA)
1201 16th St. NW, Washington, DC 20036
(202) 833-4000
website: www.nea.org

The NEA is a volunteer-based organization whose goal is to advance the cause of public education. The association lobbies legislators for school resources, campaigns for higher standards for the teaching profession, and files legal actions to protect academic freedom. At the local level, the association conducts professional workshops and negotiates contracts for school district employees. The NEA publishes *NEA Today* as well as brochures on topics such as testing, school safety, and health issues.

National Home Education Network (NHEN)
P.O. Box 7844, Long Beach, CA 90807
fax: (413) 581-1463
e-mail: info@nhen.org • website: www.nhen.org

The NHEN facilitates grassroots work for state and local home-schooling groups and individuals by providing information, networking services, and public relations on a national level. The network tracks developments in legislatures, courts, and state boards of education and helps home-schooling families set up their own legislative watch committees. NHEN publishes the *NHENotes* monthly newsletter, the *NHEN Advocacy Report*, and the *In the News Report*, which tracks print media about home schooling.

National Home Education Research Institute (NHERI)
P.O. Box 13939, Salem, OR 97309
(503) 364-1490 • fax: (503) 364-2827
e-mail: mail@nheri.org • website: www.nheri.org

NHERI is a nonprofit research organization which collects, tracks, and analyzes research on home-based education. It seeks to educate the public about home-school research through speaking engagements and through its publication of the *Home School Researcher*.

National School Boards Association (NSBA)
1680 Duke St., Alexandria, VA 22314
(703) 838-6722 • fax: (703) 683-7590
e-mail: info@nsba.org • website: www.nsba.org

The NSBA serves the national and federal needs of local school boards. The association seeks to raise awareness of school board issues, assists school boards and educators in the use of technology, reports the results of research on education issues, and lobbies Congress for funding or for reducing costly federal mandates. The NSBA publishes the monthly magazine *American School Board Journal* and the *School Board News*, a semi-monthly newspaper.

U.S. Department of Education
400 Maryland Ave. SW, Washington, DC 20202-0498
(800) USA-LEARN (1-800-872-5327) • fax: (202) 401-0689
e-mail: customerservice@inet.ed.gov • website: http://ed.gov

The purpose of the U.S. Department of Education is to ensure equal access to education and to promote educational excellence. The department provides grants to primary, secondary, and post-secondary education institutes; financial aid to students for post-secondary education; and underwrites education research. It produces hundreds of publications annually, including *Community Update*, which informs readers about available resources, services, and publications.

Bibliography

Books

David H. Albert	*And the Skylark Sings with Me: Adventures in Homeschooling and Community-Based Education.* Gabriola Island, BC, Canada: New Society Publishers, 1999.
Stacey Bielick	*Homeschooling in the United States: 1999.* Washington, DC: U.S. Dept. of Education, Office of Educational Research and Improvement, 2001.
Jennifer J. Fager	*Making Positive Connections with Homeschoolers.* Portland, OR: Northwest Regional Educational Laboratory; Washington, DC: U.S. Dept. of Education, Office of Educational Research and Improvement, Educational Resources Information Center, 2000.
John C. Holt	*Growing Without Schooling.* Cambridge, MA: Holt Associates, 1997.
Patricia M. Lines	*Homeschooling.* Washington, DC: U.S. Dept. of Education, Office of Educational Research and Improvement, 1996.
Grace Llewellyn, ed.	*Freedom Challenge: African American Homeschoolers.* Eugene, OR: Lowry House, 1996.
Mark Lorson	*Science in the Home School.* Columbus, OH: ERIC Clearinghouse for Science, Mathematics, and Environmental Education, 1999.
Isabel Lyman	*Homeschooling: Back to the Future?* Washington, DC: Cato Institute, 1998.
Roland Meighan	*The Next Learning System: And Why Home-Schoolers Are Trailblazers.* Nottingham: Educational Heretics Press, 1997.
John and Kathy Perry	*The Complete Guide to Homeschooling.* Los Angeles: Lowell House, 2000.
Brian D. Ray	*Strengths of Their Own: Home Schoolers Across America.* Salem, OR: NHERI Publications, 1997.
Mitchell L. Stevens	*Kingdom of Children: Culture and Controversy in the Homeschooling Movement.* Princeton, NJ: Princeton University Press, 2001.
Alan Thomas	*Educating Children at Home.* London: Cassell, 1998.
U.S. Education Department	*Rural Home Schooling and Place-Based Education.* Washington, DC: U.S. Department of Education, 2001.

| Jessie Wise and Susan Wise Bauer | *The Well-Trained Mind: A Guide to Classical Education at Home.* New York: W.W. Norton, 1999. |

Periodicals

Jeff Archer	"Doing It Their Own Way," *UNESCO Courier*, June 2000.
Winnie Baden	"Home Schooling Needs Checks and Balances," *New York Times*, June 25, 2000.
Shery Butler	"The 'H' Word: Home Schooling," *Gifted Child Today*, September 2000.
John Cloud and Jodie Morse	"Home Sweet School: The New Home Schoolers Aren't Hermits," *Time*, August 27, 2001.
David Gergen	"No Place Like Home," *U.S. News & World Report*, June 19, 2000.
David Guterson	"No Longer a Fringe Movement," *Newsweek*, October 5, 1998.
Andrew Herrmann	"There's No Place Like School," *Chicago Sun-Times*, October 27, 1998.
Amelia Hill	"Children Taught at Home Learn More: Youngsters of All Social Classes Do Better If They Avoid School, Study Discovers," *Observer*, August 13, 2000.
Carolyn Kleiner	"Home School Comes of Age," *U.S. News & World Report*, October 16, 2000.
Jillian Lloyd	"Home Schooling's Latest Appeal: Safety," *Christian Science Monitor*, June 4, 1999.
Isabel Lyman	"Regulators in Search of a Problem," *Perspective*, July 2000.
William R. Mattox Jr.	"Are Homeschooled Children Socially Deprived?" *Knight-Ridder/Tribune News Service*, March 3, 1999.
Peggy McCarthy	"Learning at Home, Playing at School," *New York Times*, November 16, 1997.
Helen Mondloch	"Education Hits Home," *World & I*, June 2000.
Joel Reese	"Moving into the Mainstream: Home-Schooling Is No Longer Just for Conservative Christians," *Daily Herald*, May 2, 2000.
Kevin Swanson	"Charting a Course for Home Schooling: One-on-One Environment Is Beneficial," *Denver Post*, August 29, 1999.
David Wagner	"No Place (to Learn) Like Home School," *Insight on the News*, September 8, 1997.
Pat Wingert and Barbara Kantrowitz	"Learning at Home: Does It Pass the Test?" *Newsweek*, October 5, 1998.

Index